Happy Reading!
Nick

5-19-18

Life as I Lived It

Small Town Country Living

Richard W. Block

LIFE AS I LIVED IT
SMALL TOWN COUNTRY LIVING

Copyright © 2016 Richard Block.

All rights reserved. No part of this book may be used or reproduced by any means, graphic, electronic, or mechanical, including photocopying, recording, taping or by any information storage retrieval system without the written permission of the author except in the case of brief quotations embodied in critical articles and reviews.

iUniverse books may be ordered through booksellers or by contacting:

iUniverse
1663 Liberty Drive
Bloomington, IN 47403
www.iuniverse.com
1-800-Authors (1-800-288-4677)

Because of the dynamic nature of the Internet, any web addresses or links contained in this book may have changed since publication and may no longer be valid. The views expressed in this work are solely those of the author and do not necessarily reflect the views of the publisher, and the publisher hereby disclaims any responsibility for them.

Any people depicted in stock imagery provided by Thinkstock are models, and such images are being used for illustrative purposes only. Certain stock imagery © Thinkstock.

ISBN: 978-1-4917-8776-2 (sc)
ISBN: 978-1-4917-8777-9 (e)

Library of Congress Control Number: 2016900785

Print information available on the last page.

iUniverse rev. date: 02/01/2016

CONTENTS

About the Author xi
Quote! xiii
About this Book xv

A Gift 1
Accidents 3
Air Travel 5
Animals I Have Encountered 7
Attempted Robbery 11
Beagles 16
Blackhawks 21
Blind!! 23
Bonfire 25
Bread and Jelly 29
C.P.R. Can You? Would You? 31
Can You Hear Me Now? 33
Car Crash 36
Car Show Blow Out 41
Caya Was His Name 45
Chess 49
Dad 51
Dog Bite 61
Dogs and Reasoning 65

.41 Magnum	70
Fame	71
Flag Etiquette	74
Gambling Boats	77
Getting Old	81
Ghosts	83
Grandma	88
Grandpa's Footsteps	93
Ground Zero	98
Growing Up	102
Halloween	106
Handgun Carry Permits	109
Holsters	111
Holy Smoke	115
Hoosier Hospitality	117
How I Built My House	120
I Drowned	125
Island Life, Bahamas	128
Jamaica	133
Journey to the Past	148
Just for Laughs	150
Kindergarten	152
Lace-O-Flage	155
Learning Handguns	159
Lentz	163
Life's Little Quirkes	166
Little Rock, Big Lesson	168
Magic Skunk Part I	170
Magic Skunk Part II	172
Mauser 98K	174
Memories of Summer Camp	180
Michigan Deer Season	182
Microwave Experiments	190

Miracles	193
Monkey See, Monkey Do!	196
Movies and Concerts	199
Music and Youth	202
Muzzle Blast	204
My Dog Duke	207
My First Bicycle	211
My First Job	213
My Rifle	224
My Secret Hunts	228
My Son Bubbie	230
Nature's Little Lessons	232
Neighborhood Grocery	234
New Year's Blast	237
Ozzie	239
Paw Paw Tree	241
Pete	244
Pinto Panic	246
Rabbit	248
Radios	250
Random Expressions	257
Rape	260
Rats	262
Redneck	264
Reverse Psychology	265
Ricochet	267
River Life	269
Sharp Knife	272
Sink or Swim	275
Skil	279
Snakes in the Attic	283
Some People	286
Spider Bite	288

The 4 Handgun Hunting Rules	291
The Amazing Glue	294
The Band-Aid	298
The Bank	300
The Brush Pile	302
The Bugle	304
The Bumper	306
The Cement Mixer	309
The Collection	315
The Cow Horn	317
The Crossing	320
Entertainer	322
The Flag Pole	326
The Flat Tire	330
The Handshake	332
The Name Game	334
The Nephew	337
The Owl	341
The Porcupine	345
The Problem	348
The Shrew	351
The Sky Turn	355
The Trumpet	360
The Wallet	363
The Way I See It!	366
The Whistle	368
Tom	371
Tornado	374
U.F.O.'s	380
V-65 Magna	384
Vacations	388
Water Puddle	391
West Point Pink	393

What Would You Do? 395
Wild Goose.. 397
Willie Wonderful 400
Woodlore With Dad 403

ABOUT THE AUTHOR

Colonel Richard W. Block is an Eagle Scout and a scouter for over 50 years, an avid sportsman, an instructor for the Ohio Department of Wildlife, a forth degree knight, NRA life member and instructor and works with the parents of West Point Cadets of Indiana. Colonel Block grew up in a small Indiana town along the Ohio River. This book is based on his life there as a boy and are all truc happenings.

QUOTE!

The highest badge of honor a person can wear is honesty!!

Hopalong Cassidy (Bill Boyd)

ABOUT THIS BOOK

This book is full of short stories containing common sense, knowledge, adventure and humor. These are all true stories of life's experiences, growing up in a small Indiana town along the Ohio River from the 1950's until now. Open this book and read any story that tickles your fancy. I guarantee you will learn many things from these stories. If after reading one story and you don't feel this book is for you, well then, you have read the wrong story!!

You will find this book is designed for all age groups and is very easy and entertaining reading.

Thank you in advance for purchasing my book. You won't regret it, my guarantee!!!

A GIFT

This is not a story about religion. This is a story about a gift. A wonderful gift.

I guess most people have dreamed sometime in their lives of finding a magic lamp when rubbed, would produce a genie who would grant three wishes like in a fairy tale.

Have you ever thought of what someone would wish for? I'm sure most answers would be money or wealth or long life or immortality or better living provisions. I would think that some would wish for good health or youth regained and staying forever.

Those are a lot of things to think about, but those are more than three wishes.

I think some would wish for more wishes, but that would defeat the purpose of only three wishes.

I think of this often in my fantasies or day dreams and I think I would wish for the healing power of Jesus Christ. To be able to just touch some person or child and make them healed. I see so many crippled or sick and dying people, struggling along in their everyday miserable lives and I wish I could help them be well if I had the power, even if it cost me time off my own life. Of course, I would have to be very secretive about it and anonymous as well or I would be bombarded by sick and injured people seeking my miracle cure.

What a wonderful gift Jesus had and to think how it and he were destroyed by people who could not understand what it was about. What a waste of a miraculous gift!!

ACCIDENTS

An accident is a very rare happening. Think about it. What is an accident? Well, it is just something that happens, is what you are probably thinking. But, why does it happen? What causes accidents to happen?

Hindsight is always 20/20 you know. You can look back on an accident and know that the cause was this or that and that is what caused the accident.

If you really think about it, the factor which caused the accident can be defined as negligence. That's right, negligence! Be it your own or someone else's, it all boils down to negligence on someone's part about 99% of the time, if not 100.

If someone had an accident and you were involved, you didn't have an accident you were a victim of someone else's negligence! I have always thought that the word accident is just a kind name for negligence, an excuse word that sounds nicer.

Negligence is almost always the root cause of every so call accident. Think about it for a while. Thoughts like, I neglected to drive at a safe speed. I should have replaced that weak ladder. I neglected to look up or I would have seen those power lines! I neglected to move something or put it away and that is what caused the problem. I neglected to turn the light on. If I had, I would not have stepped on or tripped over whatever.

Are you beginning to see what I am saying? Every accident has been caused by some form of negligence. I wonder if there truly is such a thing as an accident where negligence is not involved.

How am I able to prevent these happenings, you might wonder? Focus, might be a good word to describe a good start for prevention. If you make yourself more aware of what you are doing and focus on it, you might save yourself some grief at times, but no one is perfect, even though we try to be.

AIR TRAVEL

In 1968 I was drafted into the U.S. Army. Our group was to go to Fort Dix, New Jersey by plane.

I had never been on a plane before and the thought of flying terrified me at the time.

Once I flew and got over my fear, I rather liked it. In fact, I went the opposite way.

I had friends who were pilots and I would go flying with them and they would let me fly the plane whenever I wanted. Heck, its' not much different than driving a car, it's the landings that take the most skill and practice.

I've been on some pretty shaky commercial flights where people got sick and needed barf bags to puke in.

One pilot friend, Bob, used to give everyone a barf bag before boarding and tell them that they had to give it back at the end of the flight, but if they used it, they got to keep it!

Richard W. Block

My wife and I went to Germany a couple of times. It's a long flight across the Atlantic Ocean on a very large jet.

On one of the flights which travel overnight, we had a steward that was quite rude I thought. It seems he was always passing me by when they handed out the snacks and drinks.

I always had to go out of my way to get his attention to get anything from him, even though I had an aisle seat.

It naturally gets dark on those over night flights and there's really nothing to do but get comfortable and sleep. They turn all the lights down or out and it's fairly hard to resist a good nap.

Well low and behold; I see my pain in the butt steward coming down the aisle from the front of the plane toward the rear.

I see an opportunity knocking at my door, so as he passes, I stick my foot out into the aisle and trip him. He does a flying nose dive down the aisle. I pull my foot back from the isle and play possum as he looks around for whatever tripped him. It was all I could do to keep from laughing and giving myself away.

There is nothing like self-gratification to make a situation more bearable.

ANIMALS I HAVE ENCOUNTERED

It's strange sometimes, when I'm in the wilds of Michigan, surrounded by woods, fields and swamps, where nature is happening every minute of the day and it's so obvious, a lot more so than in the city, with its paved streets, many houses, traffic, people and hustle.

It's amazing how animals act around people when they have never encountered a human being before. They can't possibly realize that they are tampering with the most dangerous predator on the face of the earth! But, as long as you don't show them the error of their ways, they will continue to be fearless of you.

I think of the possum that came up to me and sniffed my boot as I stood beneath a cedar tree on a rainy deer hunting day while I was trying to stay dry and then went on his merry way as I stood still as a statue on that wet hillside.

Then there was the groundhog that came down the same cow path I was standing on, that fall day in squirrel season. I spread my feet as he drew close, just to see if he would pass between my legs. But, he stopped short and looked slowly up at me, like a kid looking at the Washington monument, starting at the foot and working his way up to the top. He then passed around me to my left and went into a dense blackberry patch where he proceeded to eat something bulbous. After he moved on I ventured over to where he was eating and found pears from an old pear tree, all grown over in the huge briar patch. When I told this story to the farmer who owned the land, he was stunned. He had lived there all his life and never knew the tree was there! Judging from the tracks beneath the tree, all the dear in the area knew it was there!

Then there was the little lost skunk walking along the road by itself. I picked him up and put him in a paper sack and took him home with me. He later stared in a magic show, where he brought down the house with his tail held high. I gave him to Bill the caretaker, where he lived in Bill's barn for a number of years, "coming and going as he well pleased," Bill always said.

Then there was the red fox that sneaked up behind me one day during squirrel season, while I was signaling my hunting buddy with my predator call, the one that sounds like a rabbit squealing. When I turned to move on, there he sat. In an instant he was gone, unlike the hair on the back of my neck which was still standing straight up! From then on I used crow calls for signaling in the woods!

Then there was the coyote that came running to my rabbit squealing predator call one moonlit snow covered night. He stopped short, a pretty good distance away and sat down, looking intently my way. I knew he could see me as

Life as I Lived It

well as I could see him. I fired a couple of shots from my pistol as he ran, just to let him know there was another predator afoot.

Then there was that darn woodpecker. He spied the shining brass Boy Scout rank pin on the front of my hunting hat as I sat high in a walnut tree, one November day during deer season. He came walking down the tree trunk looking and walking and looking and coming closer and closer. All the time he was looking very intently at the pin on my hat. He was so fascinated. He'd never seen anything like it before and he wanted it! I sat motionless watching him only inches in front of my eyes. I finally broke down and started laughing, scaring him away in the niche of time.

Then there was the porcupine that was fearless and let me pet him. With a stick of course!

But, when it comes to fearless, I have to hand it to the little chickadees. These little birds are afraid of nothing. Like the one that sat on my rifle barrel in hunting season or the one that fluttered in my face trying to land on my nose or the one that sat on my shoulder while I skinned a deer deep in the brush, waiting for a hand out of a piece of rump fat which I always hung on a bush like a suet feeder for my friends. I always enjoyed standing on the porch with a handful of sunflower seeds and the chickadees would flutter up and sit on my fingers while they picked through the seeds and flew away with a mouth full.

Richard W. Block

I could name countless more, but they know who they are and so do I, while the real mystery here is…..do you really know who you are?

You are the most dangerous predator on the face of the earth. Haven't you been paying attention???

ATTEMPTED ROBBERY

Have you ever been assaulted? I can tell you what it was like for me anyway.

In 1973, I was the closing manager at a popular fast food restaurant in Cincinnati. I liked to work the closing shift because I got to spend some time alone to do the inventory and count the money in the cash drawers before putting everything in the safe, which included the bank deposit for the next day.

While I was counting the money, the hair on the back of my neck raised up, indicating that someone was watching me.

Our rear door had a small window in it and I got up and looked out of it to check on my car. I drove a 1958 Volkswagen at the time and I always parked it where I could keep an eye on it, because parts for one that old were hard to get and people would steal parts from it if they had the opportunity.

I couldn't see anyone out there so, I resumed counting the money.

Again I felt my neck hair rise up and I felt I was being watched again, so I finished counting the drawers and the deposit and put them in the safe. I closed the safe door and spun the dial to lock it up.

Now that the money was locked up, I thought I would take a look around outside. I opened the rear door and stepped outside and stood in the doorway as the door shut behind me and I stood there quietly in the dark, listening for any kind of sound or movement. After a minute or two, I thought if there was someone here, they could only be a few feet away, around the corner, where I just happened to have a flood light burnt out and it was dark there.

I took a step to peek around the corner and sure enough, there was a young man standing there, flat against the wall as if standing on a ledge.

I thought his form looked like someone who might work here or someone I might know. It was only an quick look and my eyes were trying to adjust to the dark when he sprang upon me, throwing ether from a cup in my face and hitting me over the head with a piece of steel pipe at the same time! I didn't fall down; I just stood there looking at him in the dark, wondering what I ever did to him to make him do that to me! When he saw I had a hard head, he dropped his pipe and cup and ran like a rabbit. In an instant, he was gone.

There I stood dripping wet, wondering what he threw on me. I looked at my shirt and it was red from blood. I thought, oh crap, now I'm going to probably need stitches.

Life as I Lived It

It was then that the ether took effect and I couldn't see. I was blind!

There was an all-night restaurant just down the street and I felt my way there. As I walked in the door I asked for the manager and as I did, I could hear the customer's silverware being dropped on their plates and tables as they gasped at the sight of me. I must have looked like death warmed over, I don't know, because I couldn't see.

Someone lead me into the kitchen area, where I was handed a towel and I gave the manager my keys and asked him to lock my rear door.

I guess he also called the police and an ambulance. The news people were also there, I could feel the light heat from their camera.

I was taken to the nearest hospital where I got 6 stitches on the top of my head and my eyes were flushed out so I could see. After a while, I could see well enough to leave. I had no idea where I was and I had to ask for directions on how to get back to the restaurant. I walked about 10 blocks and when I got there, the night maintenance man was there doing his work. I looked a mess and I told him I was going home and to tell the opening manager to do the closing inventory for me.

When I got home, I put a towel on the sofa and lay down with my head on the towel so I wouldn't make a mess on the sofa. I thought I would just sleep there for a couple of hours until my wife got up for the day.

I grabbed my pistol and was sleeping with it in my hand on my chest when my wife came into the room. She let out with a scream at the sight of me; she thought I had shot myself and that I was dead!

She got a bigger shock when I opened my eyes and spoke!

She asked me what had happened to me and I told her all about it. She asked me why I was sleeping with a gun in my hand and I told her I just wanted to feel safe while I slept.

When I walked into work that night, everyone was surprised to see me there. They told me they saw me on the news last night and they thought I was dead. I guess they saw me all bloody, being loaded into the ambulance on TV.

After that, I carried a gun to work without fail and no one was aware of it.

A few days later, a detective stopped by the restaurant and talked with me. He wanted to know if I could identify the young man that had assaulted me, if he came back in a day or two with some photos.

I told him, "Yes, I could identify him". He said it sounded like this man he knew that lived nearby and was known to do this kind of crime when I described him.

The detective never returned with the photos. I guess it wasn't worth his time, but that's okay.

Life as I Lived It

That meant he was still out there somewhere and I hope he comes back. I'll be waiting.

Of course it's only been thirty plus years ago and I wouldn't recognize him now anyway.

I guess that's just the way the cookie crumbles.

BEAGLES

The Block Family has always been a dog family. We've always had dogs in our family, some purebred, some just plain mutts. But one thing is for sure, the beagle has always been the most prized of the lot. They are loving, friendly to everyone, especially children, well behaved and very intelligent.

On occasion when rummaging through boxes or old chests in the attic, I would run across old newspapers with articles about my Grandfather's award winning line of registered beagles. This was in the early 1900's vintage papers.

I fondly remember tagging along on a rabbit hunt with my Dad when I was a small boy, too young to carry a gun. There is something so captivating and fascinating about watching a well-trained beagle pursuing a rabbit.

I still remember the day, as if only yesterday, that my Dad brought home the two beagle pups and informed me that they were to be mine and that I was now responsible for their care and training. I didn't know anything about training rabbit dogs. I was only 12 years old, but I did

Life as I Lived It

know that training rabbit dogs was a lot easier if they trained with a veteran rabbit dog that played a role model from which they could learn, which I didn't have nor did I know anyone who had a good example dog for mine to learn from. When I mentioned this to my Dad, he said "That's okay, you will learn as well as you teach the dogs".

That's when I found out that I had to learn to be a rabbit dog so I could be the role model personally! This was going to be interesting, to say the least, I thought to myself.

My Dad never went afield with me, not even once. He would only give advice and pointers as time progressed. He spent most of his time making a living for our family of four. He had a stroke in his late forties and died at age 52.

Those two male beagle pups were as different as night and day. One was tall for his breed, red and white marked with green eyes. The fact that he was tall meant his legs were longer, making him fast on the run. The other was a typical beagle, black, brown and white marked, and low built, which meant he was slow and persistent.

The red and white beagle I named "Reb" which is short for rebel. The other dog my mother named "Mr. Bones" which we called Bones for short. It is a benefit to name your dog a one syllable name. The reasoning is; it makes it easier and quicker for the dog's name to be called in a repeated manner when afield.

When the dogs were big enough, I started their training. I asked my Dad, "Where do I start?" "What do I do to train these dogs by myself and with no help from another dog?"

Richard W. Block

Dad replied, "Take the dogs afield and flush out a rabbit for them. Take care to see exactly where the rabbit squat is and shove the dog's noses into it to get the scent. Then go along in the direction of flight making sure the dogs keep their noses to the ground. Every time the dog's head pops up, shove it back to the ground so he soon gets the idea and habit of always keeping his nose to the ground where the rabbit's scent is. Bark a little bit for them so they can get the impression you are on the trail of the rabbit and that's the whole idea of being the role model".

You may wonder what is a squat? It's where the rabbit has been sitting or laying for a length of time. It's generally a little hollowed out spot in a tuft of grass or an impression in the edge of a briar patch or fence row. It's a place where he hides by day and leaves from at night to feed on close by vegetation. It helps to know the habits of the animal you are after. Rabbits eat almost 24 hours a day. They live to eat. They run at night and sit by day.

They have several litters of young per year and are a very fragile animal. They run in seven year cycles, the seventh being the height of population and the rest are spent building up to the seventh year at which time, disease usually kills them off to start the cycle over again.

The rabbit is a "home body". He lives in his own little area where he knows every foot of ground, every bird nest, every sound, every smell, etc. He never ventures far.

My friend, Paul G., who lived near and was my age too, would go with me and my dogs often. Two people kicking

Life as I Lived It

out rabbits were better than one. I always told Paul that he was the best rabbit dog I ever had.

The dogs learned quick that when you called their names in such a rapid and excited manner like a machine gun rhythm, Reb, Reb, Reb, Reb, Reb, Reb, Bones, Bones, Bones, Bones, Bones, Bones, ya ya ya ya (ya-here) they knew that a rabbit has been flushed and they were on the scene instantly and without question.

Reb usually hit the trail first with Bones trailing behind. Reb was a boomer; he sounded more like a coon hound with his baying sound. Bones was a yelper, with his short high pitched yelps.

Rabbits, being a "creature of habit" and a "home body", always run in a big circle when pursed and return near their squat. All you have to do is stand still and wait and shoot him when he shows up.

If the shot is poor and the rabbit is only wounded, your well trained dog's job is to chase him down and fetch him to you after he has killed the rabbit with a bite to the ribs. And when you take that rabbit from your dog's mouth with kind soothing words and pet them both and rub their heads lavishing them with praise for a job well done, it's then that you come to appreciate all the hard work you spent and the devotion of the dogs to please their master.

I've seen times on a snowy day when the rabbits were slow and Reb was fast, that he'd catch and kill and bring me the rabbit with no shots fired.

Once you've rabbit hunted with a pair of first rate dogs, you are hooked; you don't want to go without them. There's music in the air when those dogs have a rabbit on the run.

There are times when I could care less if I ever shot the rabbit. Just watching and listening to the dogs communicate is a joy in itself!

Communicate you are wondering? Oh yes, they communicate. All animals communicate. It seems to be the nature of humans to think they are the most intelligent animal on the face of the earth.

Just remember this, if you take an intelligent human and a supposedly dumb, stupid rabbit and dump them in a remote wilderness, who will survive every time? My money would be on the rabbit.

I am sure that I am not alone when I say, "I shall miss my dogs until the day I die". I haven't rabbit hunted since.

BLACKHAWKS

My son Rich graduated from West Point Military Academy in 1999. He had asked me long before he graduated, which way should he go? Should he go Infantry, Armor, Artillery, Medical, Aviation or what?

He was in the upper percentile of his class and they offered him the chance to become a doctor, but he said no, he wanted to fly.

The Academy wanted him to stay and be an instructor on staff, but again no, he wanted to fly. I had made the comment to him earlier that it was easier to fly something home rather than drive or drag it, so he went to Fort Rucker, Alabama to flight school.

Each trainee had a "stick buddy" to train with. He used to put the toilet plunger on the floor between his knees as he sat on the sofa and used it as a control stick to practice on.

When Rich got his wings he went to Korea where the sun never shines. He did not like it there. When he rotated back to the States, he wound up at Fort Drum, New York. He would fly training missions down to Fork Polk, Louisiana.

A Blackhawk helicopter has to refuel twice on the way, so he would refuel at Wright Patterson Air Base in Dayton first, then Fort Campbell, Kentucky before landing at Fort Polk.

It so happens that our farm is in the flight path between Dayton and Fort Campbell, Kentucky and I have a fifteen acre landing field totally open and accessible to aircraft.

Rich would call ahead and we would have burgers or pizza ready and waiting for the chopper crews when they landed. The whole neighborhood would turn out for a "Block" party.

After Afghanistan, Iraq and Egypt, Rich came home to Fort Knox, Kentucky to roost before retiring.

The last time I was in a chopper was in Hawaii. A week after I left, the chopper went down in the mountains and all were killed.

Sometimes your number just doesn't come up.

BLIND!!

I am an electrician. I was working for a major restaurant franchise at the time. A call from our restaurant on Kemper Road having equipment problems, prompted me to respond to that location. While seeking out the source of the problem, I discovered a circuit breaker in one of the huge electric panels in the basement was not working. I could tell it has over-heated at some point and burnt internally; causing the problem I removed the panel face. As I was removing the damaged breaker it broke into pieces because it was so brittle, leaving debris. As I was carefully removing the debris, the electric arced across my screwdriver causing an explosion! I knew what was happening and instantly dove for the safety of the concrete floor. Even though I was lying face down with my head buried in my folded arms and my eyes tightly shut, the unbearable bright light flash still remained. It was like looking at the sun, only five times brighter.

The explosion tripped the main breaker causing a black out. All electric was out. I heard the manager shout, "What happened? Is everyone okay?" A stock boy yelled in response, "No! Dick is down and I can't tell!" I yelled, "I'm okay," but I was lying. I was blind! I yelled, "Call the electric company and have them turn everything back on, I can't do it." I found my way upstairs with help and soaked my head under the sink faucet.

Everyone was shocked to see my instant sun burnt like face with all the hair burnt away. My eye lashes were melted together. I was taken to the hospital for treatment. "You have 90% eye burn and I'll know more in a week or two when I examine you again," the doctor said. Then I was bandaged.

I had known blind people and knew a lot of tricks. I drew on my remaining senses for help. It's truly amazing how your hearing, smell and touch sharpen to a razors edge when it's their turn to run your life.

I never to this day let those senses dull, even when my sight did return. It was an ordeal that turned out to be beneficial.

BONFIRE

My Boss's home sat on four acres of ground in Western Hills, a suburb of Cincinnati.

More than half of the acreage was woods and brush. It was dense in places and he wanted to expand the lawn by cleaning out a lot of the brush and small trees or saplings.

I told him that I could rent a tractor and bush hog from the tool rental shop a couple of miles away and do it myself for him. So that is what I did.

I was very familiar with that equipment, because I had my own at my farm fifty miles away.

I rented the equipment for a day and started flattening everything within reason in the wooded area around the main lawn that faces the side street below. At one point, the bush hog swayed to one side as I was backing up and a small tree became trapped between the tractor and the bush hog. I had to get the chain saw out and cut the tree away to free up the equipment.

Richard W. Block

The next day, I returned to clean up the mess the bush hog had created. I started gathering up all the debris and putting it in a pile. Before long, I had a huge pile of brush and limbs about 10 or 11 feet high and just as big around.

My boss, Lou, asked me what I was going to do with that huge mess and I told him I was going to burn it when the time is right. He suggested I had better get a burning permit from the local fire department in Mack. So, I called the fire department up and they sent me a permit.

The pile was awful green so I let it sit and dry out a week or so. I tried to light it once, but it didn't catch fire, so I let it sit another day or two when I knew rainy weather was on the way.

I strung out water hose from the house with a squeeze nozzle on it just in case the fire tried to spread. I wet the ground around the brush pile also. I threw a couple of old tires on the pike with some kerosene and a trailing of gas to light it from a safe distance.

I lit the trail and up it went. The flames were going 20 to 30 feet high. Everything was going just as planned. All of a sudden I heard the sirens going off over in Mack where the fire department is. A car came zooming up the side street back to the neighbor's house.

I thought, I wonder what the hurry was about. I then heard someone coming through the woods from the neighbors and a man appeared in the bushes and he simply said, "Oh," and then disappeared back to where he came from.

Life as I Lived It

Well, that was kind of strange, I thought. Then I began to wonder if all those sirens were for me and the bonfire!

The next thing you know, up pulls the fire truck and the firemen are stringing out hose as a crowd of neighbors gather to watch.

The first fireman comes up the grade with the hose over his shoulder shouting orders to the other firemen below.

I said, "What do you think you are doing?" He said, "I'm going to put this fire out!" I said, "The hell you are!" At that, he looked around and saw that I had everything under control and then asked me if I had a permit to burn. I said, "As a matter of fact, I do!" He said, "Well, can I see it?" I told him that it was at the house and I would go and get it, f he would watch my fire for me while I'm gone.

I returned with the permit and he looked it over. He then told his men to pack it up and make ready to leave. The neighbor lady who called them was furious. "Are you leaving? Aren't you going to put the fire out!" she screamed. The fireman said, "No, he's doing everything right and there is no danger."

She still couldn't believe it, that they were leaving that huge fire to burn, without putting it out. I only wished I had thought to bring some hot dogs or marshmallows and been standing there roasting them when they showed up. I'd have bid them welcome to my weenie roast!

I was glad to see the rain come even though I was going to be there until the end. I kept going around the fire, shoving burnt off ends into the middle so they would burn up entirely.

I was also very glad that Lou made me obtain that permit too! That's what really saved the day!

BREAD AND JELLY

I remember when we were living on Market Street and I was just a youngster. My Mom decided to make a batch of jelly.

My Grandmother, who was my Mom's mother, made jelly every year and put it into small jars for storage purposes. When she ran out of the jars to put it in, she would use small glasses and pour melted paraphine on top of the jelly to seal it.

Well anyway, my Mom made her jelly and put it into jars like her mom always did. There is nothing like the aroma of cooking grape or blackberry jelly in the kitchen. Yum, yum. I could hardly wait to have some. I could taste it already.

Everything went right along as planned and the jelly was cooling in the jars. Soon, it was ready to eat. I popped a piece of bread in the toaster and then buttered it up while the toast was still hot so the butter would melt, in preparation for the jelly, I grabbed a jar of the jelly and shoved a spoon into it and oops the spoon wouldn't come out. It was stuck! "Hey, Mom! Look at this!" I shouted.

Richard W. Block

Mom picked up the spoon with the jar of jelly hanging onto it. Then she pulled the spoon out, but the jelly didn't let go. It hung on to the spoon in a long stringy manner like some kind of glue. Then we all started laughing. Every jar was just like the first one.

Mom's friend, Dottie from down the street, had made a loaf of bread for the occasion.

She stopped by with her loaf of fresh baked bread. Boy it smelled good. Mom showed her the jelly. Dottie said, "Oh, that's nothing. Look at this." And at that, she tried to slice her loaf of bread, but the knife couldn't penetrate it. It was like a brick.

Mom looked the situation over and said to Dottie, "You bake some more of your bread and I'll make some more of my jelly and we'll build a wall!"

My Mom had a great sense of humor. That is where I got mine I am sure.

C.P.R. CAN YOU? WOULD YOU?

The Red Cross came to my workplace one day I the id 1970's and held a course in cardio pulmonary resuscitation (C.P.R.), a great learning experience, which made me certified in its use. C.P.R. certification expired after one year, but at least I knew how to do it.

In the mid 1990's, I took the course again and learned some of the techniques that had changed slightly for better application. I was now certified again and have since kept it updated.

As an adult scouter, I teach first aid to other adults, who are just joining the scouting program. At some stage of the course I'll ask, who knows C.P.R. and there will be a show of hands. Then I'll ask of those people, who is willing to do it if the occasion arises and the number of hands are usually less.

I had thought about what my actions would be many times if the situation arose. Well it did.

It was New Year's Eve 1997; I was at my boss's vacation home in Northern Michigan. His 81 year old wife, Mary was in bed for the evening. She had Parkinson's disease and my boss had a round the clock nursing staff of two nurses to care for her. He was a very caring person of good means.

Just before the New Year hour, a nurse came running into the room saying Mary has stopped breathing. Everyone ran to her bedside. Everyone was crying in disbelief as the nurse announced "no pulse". I checked my watch to star time lapse. It's only 4 minutes to "brain dead".

I watched the staff call her name and hold her hands as time slipped away. These people are supposed to be professionals! I jumped into the middle of everything, barking orders like a Marine drill sergeant. "Get her on the floor, check for pulse and breathe!" "Nothing" was the nurse's reply. "Starting C.P.R." I barked. Two quick breaths and then the palpitations while counting aloud, over and over until I could go no more. I know in my heart that I did all I could.

How about you? Can you? Would you?

CAN YOU HEAR ME NOW?

Once upon a time in the late 1960's or the early 1970's, I worked in a distillery in the little town of Lawrenceburg, about five miles away from home. It was one of several distilleries owned by a well known company based in New York. It employed about two thousand people at its peak in our area alone.

The great thing about working a job that employs thousands of people, is the variety of people you get to spend time with, that comes from all walks of life. They can teach a young man many things about life, if he is willing to learn and if they have the patience to teach him what they know or what talent they might have.

I worked in the bottling plant which is where the whisky is bottled, labeled, cased and shipped or warehoused.

I knew hundreds of my co-workers, many of them have since passed on, but there are those that I will never forget that enriched my life many times with their stories, tips, and words of wisdom, talents and just plain friendship.

One of these people was a small fellow by the name of Bill W., whom everyone called "Willie". Bill was a relief man.

His job was to come around and take your place on the job for fifteen minutes a couple of times before lunch and a couple of times after, rotating from worker to worker each time, all day long. I usually worked on a bottling line with a lot of people so bill was on each side of me several times a day.

One day Bill was trying to get someone's attention and couldn't make himself heard above the noise of the machinery and the sounds of everything else in motion, so he whistled loud to get his point across.

I said to him, "how do you whistle like that?" I have tried to learn how to do that all my life and could never master the technique.

Bill replied, "It is fairly simple and anyone can do it with a little practice". "Show me" I said and then he showed me several different ways to whistle loud, all of which he could do.

The thumb and middle finger method, the two little fingers in the corner of the mouth and the curled tongue using no fingers at all. He could do them all!

He told me that I had to discover which technique would work best for me. Most people can only do one and no more than that.

Life as I Lived It

I felt the two little fingers in the corners of my mouth technique would be the one I could learn easiest if at all.

I practiced every day and Bill would give me pointers on how to touch my little fingers together at a wide "v" angle and how to place them on my tongue with my mouth partially open and my lips closed around them.

"Just vary the angle of your v and blow each time as you do, until you get it right", Bill said.

In about a week or two, I was whistling as loud as Bill could. I couldn't believe it!

Bill had taught me something in a couple of weeks that I had been trying to learn for most of my life!

I have used that loud whistle technique many times for many things and every time I signal with it, it brings back memories of Bill, showing me how to do it.

Thank you for being my friend!

I wish he could hear me tell him that. Bill passed on many years ago. He was a remarkable man.

CAR CRASH

In the late 1960's, I was at my friend Lanny's house, visiting his brother Larry and their parents, which I did quite often.

I was in the process of building a custom motorcycle that resembled the one Peter Fonda rode in the movie Easy Rider. I thought his bike was beautiful and I would like to have one like it.

I invited Lanny to go see it at my house, which was five miles away.

It was about 9:00 in the evening and it was dark already because we did not go on daylight savings time back then like we do now. Lanny said, I will drive, which was fine with me because he was a safe driver and I had no worries about it.

We were about half way on a straight stretch of four lane highway where there were a lot of businesses and restaurants when I saw a police car sitting on a side street watching the traffic go by.

Life as I Lived It

We were in the left lane as I pointed out the cop and asked Lanny, "How fast are you going"? Lanny looked down at his speedometer and said, "We are doing fifty", which is what the speed limit was, but as he was doing that I spied a black older model car with no lights on, sitting dead ahead in our lane. I had just enough time to yell as Lanny was looking up, "there is a car in our lane in the dark"! "We are going to hit"! I got ready for my seat belt to jerk me when I remembered I hadn't put it on like Lanny had done.

I quickly put my hands against the dash to brace myself, which was a mistake as I was soon to find out! With no time to swerve and barely enough to hit the brakes, we plowed into the rear of the black car, knocking it farther up the road. Upon impact, Lanny's seat belt held him in place, but he hit his face on the steering wheel, crushing his nose, causing it to bleed.

I, on the other hand wasn't so lucky. When I had braced myself against the dash, it was like, get ready-get set-go through the windshield!

Wham! My face- first- head hit the glass while my shins jammed under the dash, all of which caused me to bounce backwards, winding up on my knees in the seat I had been sitting in, looking out the rear window! Everything went black for an instant but came back. There I was, on my knees with my hands on my forehead, thinking wow! What a rush! I looked over to check on Lanny and he was sitting in his seat with his head back holding his bloody nose.

I looked around, still holding my head in my hands and I thought it is a wonder I didn't get cut to pieces because there was no blood on anything. I took my hands down and blood flew everywhere! I blurted out "Oh God, look at the blood"! But I put my hand over my mouth to shut myself up because I didn't want to upset Lanny, who was on a blood thinning medicine as it was.

I quickly opened the door and jumped out of the car so he wouldn't see. I went around to the front of the car, to the only working headlight, so I could see how bad I was. I was in a bent over stance and the blood was really dripping from everywhere on my head. I was wearing a brand new clean white tee-shirt and I thought to myself, "Oh well here goes my shirt", as I pulled it off and proceeded to use it for a bandage to stop the blood flow.

As I was doing all of this, the police are pulled around behind us and turned on his lights while calling for an ambulance and this kid came running up to me saying "I am sorry, it's my fault. My battery is dead". I looked at him and said,

"Get away from me kid. If it wasn't for the cop sitting here, I would break your neck and say the crash did it! "At that, he promptly left, and I didn't see him anymore.

The ambulance arrived and we got in while the police were trying to ask me all kinds of questions, which were delaying our departure. I said to come up to the hospital and ask there, we needed to go. I was worried about Lanny; I knew something was wrong with him.

We were transported to our local hospital where I called Lanny's parents to come and see what was going on with

Life as I Lived It

him. The hospital people said he only had a broken nose and he was okay. Lanny's parents took him out of there and to the hospital in Cincinnati where it was determined he was bleeding internally and would have been dead by morning if he would not have come there for further evaluation and care!

I, on the other hand, called my family doctor, to come and sew me up in the hospital emergency ward. His name was Doctor Baker and I kept him in practice sewing me up throughout my young life.

As I sat in a hallway on a chair waiting for the Doc to show up, this elderly nurse kept pestering me to see my cut on my head under the tee-shirt bandage I had improvised and was holding in place. I kept telling her to go away; I will get glass fragments in my eyes if I remove the bandage. But, she kept pestering me to show her and I kept telling her to go away and leave me alone. She finally tugged at my shirt and glass pieces fell out and I couldn't see. I shouted at her in anger that if I could see her to get my hands on her I would kill her on the spot. She left and never came back.

Shortly thereafter, Dr. Baker came to my rescue and they put me on a table where he put some 30-40 stitches in my face and head. After he got finished sewing up my head, a young nurse was cleaning me up with a damp cloth, when I asked him if he was done and he said, "Yes". So I propped myself up on my elbows on the table and pulled up my pant legs and said do you mind sewing up my legs before you leave? He looked at me with amazement and said, "Didn't they check you over when you came here?" I said, "No, they didn't even offer me a band-aid. If I hadn't been conscience, I would have bled to death.

As the Doc was about to sew up my legs, one of the life squad members offered to pull off my boots, saying I would be more comfortable if he did. I said, "No, you leave those boots right where they are, I am going to need them to escape just as soon as the Doc is done sewing me up"! The nurse immediately said, "Aren't we going to keep him overnight?" Dr. Baker replied, "No, if he wants to go, you let him go!" He was a great man and he knew me well.

I called up a waitress at a restaurant I knew and asked her to please come and get me and bring me something to wear because I used all my clothes for bandages. I went home in a beach towel!

CAR SHOW BLOW OUT

As a teenager, one of my favorite events was the Cavalcade of Customs Car Show, held at the convention center in Cincinnati each year. It's a two day event on a Saturday and Sunday mainly.

I try not to tell this story very often because it's hard to tell it in its entirety without laughing myself into tears, but I'll try to write it, so here it goes.

I remember vividly, I was 19 years old and had just gotten married. I had been sick all week and had diarrhea so bad that I couldn't get far enough away from the toilet to even watch TV.

The car show was going on and I was "chomping at the bit" to go and see it. I never missed the car show and it was Sunday, the last day of the show already.

I was feeling better, so we decided we'd go. I was happy to get out of the house. We drove to Cincinnati, bought our tickets and entered the giant show floor of the convention center with its long rows of custom cars and motorcycles on display. The place was crowded as usual, everyone drinking beer and eating hot dogs while viewing all the fine cars. It was always an exciting event for me. I had built a custom motorcycle and wanted to enter it in the show sometime in the near future, so I was kind of searching for information as well as looking at the displays for pointers.

We were at the far end of the floor when it hit me. I had to go to the restroom! And I had to go now! I wasted no time wading through the crowd of people making my way to the restroom at the other end of the floor.

I entered the restroom with its dozen or more toilet stalls and as many urinals to find they were all occupied, except for one, into which I hurried.

The toilet was a mess. You know how it is at an event where beer is served and no one lifts the seat before using the john because they don't care and their aim is poor especially after a few beers.

There's no way I could sit on that toilet and no time to clean it up either. I had to go now! I was ready to explode this instant! The toilet was unusable, but I had no choice except to just squat over it and not sit on it.

I could barely get my pants down in time and get over the toilet before I lost control of my puckering ass hole. Instead of the big squirting sensation, I got a big wet ka-pow blast that probably made the Richter scale!

Because I was in a half standing position, I could feel stuff running down the backs of my legs and dripping off my

Life as I Lived It

body parts. Thank goodness most of it came out on the first blast, because just a few more spurts and I was ready for the paperwork.

It took a while to clean myself up to say the least but I was in a hurry to get away from the smell and mess. About the time I was cleaning off my shoes, a couple of young men came in the restroom and one of them had to use a toilet, but all were occupied. He kept pacing back and forth along the row of toilets, announcing rather loudly that he wished someone would hurry up because he had to use a toilet right away.

I waited until he reached the other end to slip out of the stall and over to the hand sinks without being seen. Suddenly his buddy yelled, "look, there's an empty stall, grab it!"

I'm watching in the mirror as the young man ran into the stall and closed the door behind him. I could see his feet freeze in their tracks as he turned and saw the toilet. Then he shouted to his buddy, "Holy shit! You ought to see this! I can't use this one, its trashed!" Then he started to describe in detail.

"It looks like a shit bomb went off in here! There's shit on the walls, on the floor, all over the toilet, even on the toilet paper dispenser! It's a total mess except for the tow footprints in front of the toilet!

A crowd was gathering as I slipped out the door with my hand over my mouth so they couldn't hear me

43

laughing. It looked like they were viewing a Rembrandt or something.

By the time I reached the end of the floor again, the maintenance crew had closed the restroom for repairs.

I think this was the last show I went to there.

CAYA WAS HIS NAME

The first time I saw Caya, he was just a puppy that my sister-in-law and her boyfriend had gotten somewhere. It was a Norwegian Husky they told me.

I took one look at his feet and I knew that little puppy was going to be a good sized hound when it grew up! It was white with some brown and black patches of color on his short hair coat. I wondered what would be in store for Caya when he out grew the apartment that he was living in.

About a year later that question was answered when I saw Caya at my old house where my ex-wife and children now lived.

Caya was on a chain in the backyard, with all the grass worn away where he had a limited amount of room to move around. I felt sorry for him because that is no life for a dog that's born to run.

On one of my visits, my ex asked me if I wanted the dog and I said no, I don't need a dog and besides, the dog has had no association with me and may not like me, being I am a stranger and all.

She told me that if I didn't take the dog, she was going to take it to the dog pound. The County dog pound was a filthy death camp for dogs because I had seen it once.

A friend of mine, who didn't like it either, went over there after dark and cut a hole in the fence, letting all the animals out. It took the dog warden several days to round up most of the escaped animals.

I finally agreed to take Caya to my farm. I had 150 acres that I didn't lose in the divorce and I had built a house for myself to live in.

I let Caya run free. He was in Heaven! No more chains for him, he was his own master. Cays soon learned the boundaries of the entire farm and rarely left the property. Every day Caya would escort me out the quarter mile driveway and would be waiting to escort me back when I returned in the evening from work.

I clocked him running alongside my car several times. Caya could run 30 miles per hour at his top speed. That's fast.

The farm was his domain and he protected every inch of it. Caya would kill any other animal that dared come on the place. I found other dogs and cats and any other animal he could catch. I saw him catch and kill a groundhog one day and it only took seconds for him to do it.

Life as I Lived It

My neighbor lady brought her dad to the house one day to see what I had built. I heard her screaming outside to come quick that Caya was attacking her father! I ran out of the house to see what was going on and Caya had her father pinned against the side of the house and wouldn't let him move! He didn't bite or harm the man, but just let him know he wasn't to move!

Caya had never been aggressive toward any human being before. He was a good judge of character though and I knew he sensed something wasn't right and he was protecting us from that. I called Caya off and no harm was done. Later on we found out the man was a child molester and went to jail for a few years.

I never worried about my children's' safety when they were at the farm because I knew they were under Caya's watchful eye when they were outside of the house.

No one went anywhere around the farm without Caya's escort. He was always there, whether you were picking berries or fishing in the creek.

Caya was fearless which proved to be his down fall.

One night he got into a scrap with a pack of coyotes. One on one is no problem, but 3 or 4 one is impossible. Caya had met his match and the coyotes tore him up pretty bad, but he still made it home in one piece.

After that he stuck close to the house at night and when the coyotes were out, he would stand on hi hind legs, looking in the window, wanting to come inside. After

Caya's wounds healed, he started having seizures which eventually killed him.

Caya was one of the greatest dogs I ever had the pleasure of knowing. Caya wasn't a pet, he was family.

CHESS

Chess…..Now there's a game!!!...Or is it? Is it really a game?

I suppose there are those that think it's just a game and for those that do, I feel sorry. They would have to be some of the most naïve people in the world.

What then, is Chess all about?

What is Chess? WHAT…IS….CHESS?!!!!

The meaning of what Chess boils down to three little words. "Chess is Life." That's right; chess is all about the struggle to prevail in life's various situations. It's about solving problems, strategy, sacrifice and gain, making the right move and at the right time.

How many times have you heard the phrase, "Making the right move," or "that was a good or smart move," when someone did something beneficial? Well, those remarks stem from moving chess pieces on a chess board.

Chess dates back to the Roman Legion period and prevails yet in today's military and its strategies. Chess pieces come in many configurations. The chess pieces that depict soldiers, usually the era of "knight of old," are more beneficial in a military sense then the regulation configuration of chess pieces.

When you lose one of these pieces to your opponent, you've lost a soldier, not just a game piece. It makes you more aware of your mistakes and/or your sacrifices when you're losing people and not just pieces.

Let' look at the game board, it has 64 squares. One half of these squares are black. The other half are another color such as red, grey, brown or white, but black is always the color of one half of the squares.

When the board is set properly in front of you, a black square will be the number one square on your left and the number eight square on your right will be the other color, usually red or white.

The board has 8 squares from left to right and 8 squares from front to rear, a total of 64 squares.

The 8 rows of square from left to right are known as ranks.

The 8 rows of squares from front to rear are known as files.

You've heard of ranks and files. Well guess where that comes from!

DAD

My Dad was born in the year 1916. He was to be the eldest of five children, his mother dying in childbirth with the sixth child who died with her as well. She was buried with the boy baby in her arms. My Dad and his oldest sister Margie had to take care and raise their younger brother and sister in place of their mother. The fifth child, Betty, was adopted out to another couple because it was too difficult to take care of that many children.

Many years later though, Betty and her new husband "popped up" after the war and be part of the family again. I don't know if Betty ever got to meet her father because he died shortly after the war ended in 1945.

During the depression Dad worked in a bakery for a short time. He would sweep up the flour off the bakery floor, dirt and all and use it. It is hard to visualize life being so tight unless you have been there. Dad said they lived off the game they hunted to carry them through.

By the time the war came around, Dad was working as a projectionist in a movie theatre in the next town. His Dad, my Grandfather, was a projectionist in their home town of

Richard W. Block

Aurora at the Grand Theatre. There were no televisions in those days and all the people would go to the movie theatre once a week or more to catch up on the news and to see a movie which was mostly silent.

A music script came with the movie which would be played on a piano by someone while the movie was running on the screen. I understand that my Grandfather was the piano player and entertained as well between features. I also understand that my Father played the piano as well, but I never knew it. His sister, my Aunt Mae told me this year after my Dad's passing.

When the war came, Dad and his brother, Lloyd went into the Army. Lloyd went into the Army Air Corp and was stationed in the Aleutian Islands across from Russia on the tip of Alaska. Dad was in the 83rd Division Signal Corp.

Dad hit the beach in France on D-day and fought all the way to Berlin and the wars end. He was wounded three times and received the Bronze Star.

He rarely talked about it much unless he had a few drinks and loosened up a little. Dad said he wouldn't take a million dollars to go through that war again, but he wouldn't take a million dollars to have missed it either.

My old Scoutmaster, Buck Crontz, told me he first met my Dad at Camp Atterbury, Indiana during his basic training. It was movie night and everyone was dressed according to code except for one guy, which was my Dad, who was wearing fatigues. Buck went up to him and told him he had better change his clothes or he was going to get into

Life as I Lived It

trouble. My Dad told him NO, because he was the only projectionist and without him there would be no movies, so he could get away with doing pretty much as he pleased.

Dad told me he used to go to the armory and get a .22 cal. training rifle and go squirrel hunting on base. He would have one of the cooks fry them up for him for supper. He must have had the powers to be over a barrel somehow, because he seemed to be able to do as he pleased whenever he wanted to do something.

In one of Dad's talking sessions he told me that when his unit was in the landing craft on its way to hit the beach, his lieutenant stuck his head up to see what was going on and a shell took his head off. From that time on, Dad was in charge and he ran everything because he was the First Sergeant. He said that some time later on he was given a new Lieutenant, but he was so scared he couldn't handle it and he broke down and was taken away and never replaced.

I can only imagine why, because Dad was in the Signal Corp and they were always out in front, stringing phone lines for communications. It was one of the most dangerous jobs. The next officer above Dad was a Captain, who rarely ever came up to the front. Dad said he was a real chicken shit and he hated him with a passion.

They were supposed to have a push but it was called off. The Captain didn't bother to tell Dad, so Dad took 30 men across a river on the night before the push was suppose to happen to set up communications and lay phone lines. They were to wait there and join the troops in the morning when the push started. When daylight came and there was no battle, the Germans cut them to pieces because they were all alone left hanging out in the breeze so to say.

Only five men made it back across the river. Dad lost 25 men because of the Captain. I think if he could have gotten hold of him, he would have killed him.

The 83rd Division was known as the Rag Tag Circus. They were known for capturing enemy vehicles and using them against the enemy. The 83rd wound up as part of Patton's 3rd Army. They raced across Europe and Dad was there.

Dad lost three jeeps in one week. When he called the motor pool for a 4th one, the Sergeant said, "I am coming up there to see what is going on!" When he got there, Dad's unit was behind a bombed out farm house relaxing like nothing was going on. The sergeant asked dad where is your jeep and what is wrong with it. Dad said it is right out there in the middle of the field, go and see if you can do anything with it!

So, the Sergeant rounded the corner of the building and headed out to where the jeep was sitting, not knowing that the Germans had a machine gun set up in the woods on the other side of the field, which was the reason everyone was behind the old farm house. It was kind of a joke on the motor pool Sergeant who was a pain in the butt to get anything from. Well, the Germans opened up, spraying bullets everywhere at the Sergeant who came crawling back around the corner of the building unharmed but scared shitless. "I will send you down another jeep", was all he said as he scrambled away back to the motor pool.

Life as I Lived It

I asked Dad what had happened to the jeep in the field and he told me the Germans shot it to pieces and it caught fire and burnt.

Dad had every weapon you could think of, but his favorite was a 1903 Springfield with a scope on it. He said he could split hairs with that rifle but he told me to never use a rife like that in combat because someone always screws with it behind your back and when you need it the most, you can't hit anything with it. He said he had just previously sighted it in when he got into a scrape. He said he had to look down the side of the barrel to hit the German that had him pinned down. That was the first and only time he admitted killing an enemy. After he said that he shut up and wouldn't talk anymore about it.

He captured a German Luftwaffe Colonel who was all dressed up with his bag packed ready to surrender. Dad said he busted him in the mouth, knocking him down in the mud and took his weapons away and sent him back as a prisoner. Dad really hated the Germans even though it is our family heritage.

Dad said he just missed getting Rudolf Hess. He entered his mountain lodge and the food was still warm on the dining room table, so they sat down and ate the meal. The Germans had a lot of mountain hunting lodges and Dad went through a lot of them. They were all stocked with any kind of gun you could imagine.

Dad said it broke his heart to have to destroy all those fine hunting guns. They would take them out and wrap them around a tree, busting them to pieces. Dad said he found a Browning shotgun that shot so sweet, he didn't have the heart to destroy it, so he took it apart and wrapped it in his raincoat and carried it halfway across Europe until he could get the chance to send it home.

When Dad returned home after the war, he gave that shotgun to "Uncle Harry Watts", who won many shooting matches with it. Harry was a trap shooter.

At the war's end, Dad was out and about in his jeep enjoying the peace I guess and when he returned he found his men digging a latrine. He asked what was going on and he was told that some officer stopped by and told them to dig a latrine. Dad said to stop digging and go get some explosives and blow the hole for the latrine, which is what they did. Well, the next thing you know, here comes the MP's (Military police) in a jeep wanting to know who gave the order to blow the latrine. Dad spoke right up and said he did, his men weren't going to waste their time digging a hole. The MP's told Dad to get in the jeep, that he was in big trouble and they were taking him to the Provo Marshal's headquarters.

So, Dad bid an unusual farewell to his men and left with the MP's. The Provo Marshal was very unhappy about the blasting of the latrine hole and he was telling Dad that the German people were our friends now and that he didn't want to start the war all over again and that he was going to court marshal Dad and make an example out of him! Dad spoke right up and said, "No you are not!" "You are not going to do a damn thing to me or anybody else!" The Provo Marshal said, "What do you mean by that?" Dad said, "Have you looked out of your window lately?" At

Life as I Lived It

that, the Provo Marshal went to the window and looked out. Dad's men had set up machine guns and had the place surrounded.

Dad then said, "If I am not out of here in five minutes, my men are going to open up and level this place and kill everyone in here." At that, he walked out, leaving them all with their mouths hanging open in disbelief! Nothing ever became of the incident.

Fed up with everything, Dad decided it is time to go home, so they loaded up all their gear in trucks and headed to the coast, got on a ship and came home, with orders only catching up with them at the boat dock!

After arriving in the U.S.A., he boarded a train for home to Indiana, which would take him to Cincinnati, the closest train station to home. On the train, a man came through announcing that anyone caught with government property would be prosecuted. The officers had taken their .45 colt pistols with them and were in a bind as what to do with them. Dad said to just throw them in his duffel bag if they wanted to get shed of them, so they did.

I asked Dad if they really searched for stuff and he said yes they did. Well how did you keep them from finding them? He said he was using his duffel for a seat and he sat on it and they didn't search it.

After the train stopped, the officers wanted their pistols back, but Dad claimed he didn't know anything about them, but he could call a MP over to see about them. Dad had seven pistols when he got home, which he gave away to friends.

He had no use for the Army .45 because you couldn't hit anything with it.

Dad had an experience in the war where he was stringing wire across a field and a German Soldier shot at him and he jumped up and took off running. Dad's rifle was in the jeep, too far away to get to, so he pulled out his .45 and shot once, twice, three times, then emptied the gun at him and then throwing the gun at him, saying well, so much for that.

Dad worked at the local distillery for a while, where he didn't get along with his cocky supervisor. So, one day he decided he had enough of this jerk and he up and busted him in the mouth, knocking him on his butt, which got Dad fired.

Dad was a no nonsense type of person and you didn't mess with him. He worked at various jobs and one of them was maintaining the projectors at the movie theatre. He would show the whole movie and I would be the only person in the theatre to watch it. I enjoyed watching him clean the projectors and watching movies with him.

He was always working, trying to make a dollar to raise his family. Sometimes I think he worked himself into an early grave.

We used to do a lot of family camping with friends and relatives. I think camping was a habit with Dad after spending all those years in the war.

Life as I Lived It

Dad bought me a Winchester youth .22 rifle when I was 10 years old to hunt with. Of course, it would go camping with me too. I would go out and shoot squirrels, birds, bottles, cans and such. One day I was doing just that, up the gravel road from our camp, when this man in a pick-up truck stopped and asked me what I was doing. I told him I was just shooting a few birds. He wanted to know where my parents were and I told him just down the road camping. He said he owned this place and marched me down the road in front of his truck, back to camp. He and my Dad had words and after he left, Dad scolded me for letting that man get the better of me. He told me to never let anyone push me around when I have a rifle in my hand, no matter how big or old they are.

At the time I thought that to be a little farfetched, but now I appreciate his advice.

When I got into cub scouts, my Dad and Mom both were involved. My Dad would make the awards with plaster casts which he hand painted. He along with the Cub master and another adult or two, took all the cub scouts camping for the week end at Versailles State Park. It was a great time. We had a big campfire and lots of fun. I guess we were a little too noisy for some of the neighboring campers, because one of them came over to our camp the next morning to complain. He got in my Dad's face and was a little too rude. That was a big mistake. You guessed it. Wham! One punch and the man lay on his back, holding his jaw and wondering what had hit him. He got up and left only to return with the park ranger who told us we had to leave. What a cry baby that guy was.

Richard W. Block

Dad had a stroke in his late 40's, but he still got around with a cane. It affected his right side and his speech as well.

Dad liked to go to all of the bars in town and have a drink or two. Dad and Mom owned a bar themselves so they knew everyone in town that ran a bar as well. All of the bars had bowling machines and they all had a bowling team to compete with other bars. They would rotate from bar to bar with the bowling competition, which was great for business.

I always knew which place Dad was at because our dog Brownie would always be out front hanging around, keeping an eye on the ole' man. Brownie was left behind by a family that moved out of town to fend for his self. I always liked the dog but Dad didn't want him around. As time went on, Dad and Brownie became inseparable pals.

As Dad and Brownie grew old, Dad would tell me that someday I was going to have to put Brownie down. It never happened that way though. In November of 1967, Dad passed away in his sleep. Brownie laid on the porch howling and howling until he mourned himself to death. I guess he went with him.

DOG BITE

My friend Jerry M. raised St. Bernard dogs as a hobby. He loved those dogs with a passion and they loved him as well.

They say that dogs resemble their masters more often than not.

I just thought I would throw that in and say no more on that statement.

I remember the day one of his male dogs got loose and was killed on the highway by a passing car. Boy was he mad about it. He was even madder when he found he was responsible for damages to the car and had to pay the car owner, rather than be paid for his god loss.

The car might as well hit a cow; a St. Bernard is a big heavy built dog!

Jerry had worked out a deal where he had rented several rooms in a school that had moved to a new location and left the old one in good repair.

Richard W. Block

I stopped by one cold winter day to check on some equipment he was repairing for me at work. His St. Bernard, named Sherman, was tethered on a long cable which ran from the building to a big maple tree about thirty yards away.

Sherman was a one man dog, devoted solely to Jerry. I knew Sherman and I was friendly with him on many occasions. He was on the far end of the cable by the tree and I paid him no mind as I knocked on the big double doors of the old school house. I usually had to knock for a while for Jerry to hear me above the radio that was always playing and the door to his room down the hall distance as well.

I was glad I had my coveralls on because it was a little cool and it usually took Jerry a while to get to the door. Sherman came trotting up and sat at my feet. I looked down at him and kept knocking on the door. Sherman nudged me with his nose on my waist like he wanted me to pet him.

I didn't trust Sherman when Jerry wasn't present, so I held my arms and hands about shoulder high so Sherman would understand that I was not going to pet him as I thought that was what he wanted.

As I knocked again, Sherman bit me on the leg vertically, up and down, not crossways like biting an arm, where my left pants pocket was. He bit in deep almost to the bone and hung on like a snapping turtle not about to let go! He couldn't get his mouth all of the way closed because in my pants pocket was four sets of keys and in my coverall pocket was a screw driver and other items which were

Life as I Lived It

all inside Sherman's mouth preventing it from closing. He could have taken a serious chunk of meat out of me otherwise.

I smacked the dog on the head but he held his grip with no result. I instantly reached in my right pants pocket and pulled out my pocket knife intending on cutting the dog's throat in the next instant.

I stopped myself in the nick of time with the thought of Jerry killing me for killing his dog! At that moment, someone was at the door inside yelling foe Jerry to come quick!

I had both my hands in Sherman's mouth trying to pry his jaws open and free myself when Jerry arrived.

A St. Bernard has a head like a bear and just as powerful. I was having no luck. Jerry punched the dog in the forehead with his fist as hard as he could several times and still the dog held his grip. Jerry is a pretty big guy too! Those punches would have knocked a human being out!

Jerry said, "Get your hands out of his mouth and let me get mine in there and I'll see if I can do any better".

Jerry tried to open Sherman's mouth but could make no headway. Finally Jerry just pulled Sherman's head from my leg, blood ran into my boot as Sherman's jaws snapped shut on Jerry's hands breaking one of his fingers in the process. I jumped into the Company truck and Jerry yelled, "Where are you going?" I yelled back, "to the lumber yard!"

Richard W. Block

The lumber yard was owned and ran by people I'd grown up with and knew most of my life. I did a lot of business there. I came through the door and headed for the restroom. As I passed the sales counter I told the guys, "I've been hurt bad, you know what I need!"

One of the guys yelled, "Block's hurt again, send a tube of super glue to the restroom quick."

I dropped my pants and glued my leg back together.

Later on, I asked Jerry why he thought Sherman attacked me. Jerry's only reasoning was that some dogs are very territorial and that Sherman felt I was infringing on his territory.

A few months later, Sherman bit a person in an alley in downtown Cincinnati tearing the man's pants to pieces but doing no harm to the man. Shortly after that, Sherman died. Jerry was heartbroken, I had mixed emotions.

I had nothing to do with it, really!!!!

DOGS AND REASONING

People, who are not dog lovers or dog oriented, probably never stop to think, that each dog has its own personality, just the same as humans do.

Dogs can love you and be you're most devoted and faithful friend for life or they can dislike you and never be of any significance to you forever.

At this point you may think that just about sums it up, but there is a grey area in between and that is where this story lies.

The grey area is where you have dogs that can't make up their mind, whether they want to be your friend or you're enemy. They are in a state of distrust. They are shy, timid, elusive and untrusting of most all human beings they come in contact with.

There is an exception though, children.

Dogs most generally relate to children for some reason, no matter how shy and distrustful the dogs personality is. I've always felt that the dog considers children as harmless, even when the child is pulling the dogs tail or ears or being too rough in some similar manner, the dog just stand there and takes the abuse willingly.

Just let an adult try that. It's not going to happen. That same distrustful dog is not going to let you even get close enough to pet him. He darn sure isn't going to come if you call him, but just let a child reach out his hand and the dog is right there, providing there is no adult close by.

Dogs were always straying in at my farm and seemed to find a home with my family.

One female hound mated with the neighbors chow and produced puppies. After most were found homes, we wound up with two male pups which looked nothing alike. One looked like a shaggy sheep dog and the other looked like his chow father.

My son mike took a liking to the one that looked like a chow. Mike would play rough with him, teaching him to be aggressive and mean.

Mike created an alpha dog. I think he did this because he missed a previous dog we had, that had died and he wanted another dog that was similar, to rule the neighborhood like the other alpha had done for several years previous.

Mike was the only person who could handle him. I couldn't even get close enough to even pet him or any of the other dogs as well.

Life as I Lived It

Mike's dog would get first choice of the food set out for all of the dogs and fight the others off until he had his fill or someone chased him away.

One day in the fall, I decided to pour a concrete porch slab at the west end of the house. The truck came in the late afternoon and it took us until almost dark to get the concrete finished out.

The great thing about pouring and finishing concrete around dark is that, leaves do not fall off the trees after dark due to the calmness of the nighttime. As a result, you won't have leaf patterns in the face of your wet concrete for eternity. You didn't know that, did you?

Well, what did concern me, was the dogs!

I just knew those darn dogs would be in that fresh concrete as soon as I turned my back.

I figured if I could subdue the alpha dog, the others would be no trouble, so I told Mike to catch his dog and chain him up beyond the other end of the house, where we had a dog house with a chain that would hold him.

Mike's dog had never been tied up before. It was a new experience for him to say the least.

He would run and when he reached the end of the chain, he would do a flip with a jerk, landing on his back, only to pick himself up and go again in a different direction with the same result. He kept doing this time and time again, while yelping and whining all the while.

Richard W. Block

I sat in a lawn chair until dawn, guarding over the fresh concrete until it was hard enough that it could not be damaged by dogs walking on it.

Mike's dog had finally settled down after countless hours of fighting with the chain. I guess he finally got worn out and gave up.

I decided that I might as well turn him loose, now that the concrete was hard enough.

I walked up to him as he lay there, talking to him in a soothing, reassuring tone of voice. I pet him and made over him as I removed the chain from around his neck. All of a sudden, he realized he was free! He was jumping and running all around in such a joyous manner, with the energy of ten dogs.

It had been many years since I had seen a dog that happy to be free. It reminded me of a time long past. When I would appear, with gun in hand, and my dogs knew they were going hunting. I would set them free and they would display a fury like no other, of boundless energy eager to "show their stuff."

Mike's dog was no exception; however, there was a difference.

My status of being in the distrustful grey area had now been upgraded to "savior and best friend!"

What a change of heart! I could call and he would come. I could make over him and show my affection, which he gladly warmed up to!

We were best of friends from then on.

Guess who took my place in the grey area?

Poor mike. After all, the way the dog saw it, Mike's the one who put that awful chain on him!

.41 MAGNUM

I think it was he,
my old man,
who said I was born
with a gun in my hand.

I learned to shoot,
young as a teen.
My eyes were sharp,
my skills were keen.

I never shot twice
Whenever I shot,
I only shoot once,
to kill what I want,
so woe is he
who faces my gun
it's death to him, so barks my forty one.

I've killed deer and wild hogs,
with some help from the dogs,
from the forty one flame.

It does not roar
Like a forty- four,
It does not offend.
It's my best friend.

FAME

Being famous like a movie star is not as great as one might think.

I suppose everyone, at one time or another has wished they were a star or a well-known personality, recognized by everyone, everywhere they may go.

People tend to wish these things because it is something that looks exciting and glamorous, a dream come true, something they have never experienced.

It is kind of funny how it all starts out in that very manner, but as time goes on, the excitement and glamour wears away to just being a routine, "life in the eyes of the public". Suddenly, the dream has become a nightmare. Your life is not your own anymore, it is governed by your fans.

I know several personalities. At first, it is fun and exciting to be around them, watching all their fans making all over them, asking for autographs, shaking their hands, hugging and kissing them and jumping up and down with excitement. WOW!

That is fine for a while, but there will come a time, when a breaking point is reached and all of this attention becomes a nuisance.

I spent some time chauffeuring a top N.F.L. quarterback and several other team players to various places and events.

At first, it was kind of "exciting", just to be "hanging out" with these guys. As time went on, it became "interesting" to be around these well-known sports figures.

In the end, I felt sorry for these people because their popularity gave them no time to themselves to be a normal human being and do as they pleased.

I remember eating at a crowded restaurant and people would come up to the table with items in hand asking for autographs. I was surprised at the abrupt,

"No, we are trying to eat a meal here!" reply.

At first, I thought they were very rude to these loyal fans who only wanted an autograph from such a famous person, that they would probably never encounter so easily again.

After a while, I realized that when you are that popular, you have to draw the line at some point in time and simply say "no". Enough really does become enough.

I know for a fact that these football players, could have taken a different girl to bed every night, but they turned them away instead!

Life as I Lived It

Beautiful young and sexy women would virtually throw themselves at these players, only to be turned down. Hard to believe isn't it?

To this day, I have never lost my respect for these people because they earned it many times over.

Now let us take a look at Elvis Presley.

Here is a man so popular and identifiable, that he could not even go out in public without a force of bodyguards!

Can you imagine not being able to even go to a grocery store without being mobbed by fans? Elvis had to rent an entire movie theatre just to see a movie. Even then, he was accompanied by a thirty person staff. I have heard it say, that he could not even go to the restroom without security on hand.

I am sure Elvis longed to be free of all of this and just be a regular person, able to walk the streets and go unnoticed once again, just as it was before he became so popular.

I wonder if he even remembered what it was like to enjoy this freedom?

FLAG ETIQUETTE

The other day at work, one of our salesman, Steve, approached me and asked me if I knew anything about flag etiquette. (This being the day after the September 11, 2001, terrorist attack on New York).

I, being an Eagle Scout, a bugler and an adult scouter of 40 plus years said, "Yes, I know everything about flag etiquette. What would you like to know?"

Steve asked, "When do you put it up and when do you take it down? What about leaving it up all night like some do, and what if it is raining?"

I replied, "Hoist it up rapidly at sunrise, and lower it slowly at sunset. Leave it up all night if it has a dedicated light, not just a street light or nearby light, and take it down in foul weather.

I was happy to answer Steve's questions with answers that I knew to be correct.

You know after the September 11, attack I never in my life saw so much abuse to the meaning of flag etiquette in the U.S.A.

Life as I Lived It

Patriotism is at an all-time high, which is absolutely great!!!!

There are flags flying everywhere, homes, businesses, cars, trucks, buses, motorcycles, etc. The list can go on forever, not mentioning decals, stickers, pennants, bunting, pins and shirts.

I was traveling down the street after work, headed for home when I saw an American flag lying beside the road as I have been seeing frequently lately, a lot of the same. It was one of those roll it up in your window mounts on a plastic stick that is the big fad now days.

I thought, I can't leave that lay there like that. It's not right. You'd think that the person that lost it would have stopped and picked it up at the very least. Maybe they weren't aware of its disappearance. So I turned around and headed back. Just as I was getting to the scene of the crime, the car ahead of me pulled to the side, the driver jumped out, ran across the lanes of traffic and picked up the flag and returned to his car.

I felt a sigh of relief to know that I was not alone when it came to showing respect for the symbol of a great nation.

It is great to see the patriotic enthusiasm that is abounding everywhere today. It's sad that it takes a disaster to spur it on. It is also sad to see people displaying flags that they haven't had out for years that are faded, tattered, torn, shredded, dirty or obsolete and are proud as a peacock to be displaying that rag, I mean flag. It's a crime that they have no idea what an embarrassment their display of the American flag is.

To set the record straight, only flags in good to new condition should be flown. They should not be faded, tattered or worn in any manner.

It is not acceptable to fly or display a dirty flag. It should be replaced not washed. Dry cleaning is the proper procedure, I have been informed.

The proper disposal of a flag that is no longer serviceable is by burning or burying, burning being the preferred method. If you want it burnt by ceremony, give your flag to your local American Legion or Boy Scout Troop and they will dispose of it for you in a befitting manner.

Don't be afraid to speak up when you see an infraction of flag etiquette because if the proper etiquette is not made known, the problem will never be corrected.

GAMBLING BOATS

Gambling has always been illegal in the state of Indiana as well as the surrounding states too. Gambling has always been there anyway though in the form of card games and slot machines, but low keyed and behind closed doors.

If you really wanted to gamble, you could go across the river to Kentucky and play the horses at any of several race tracks. Horse racing has always been a big business there.

Speaking of the river, guess what, a loop hole in the gambling laws surfaced!

All of a sudden, gambling of all kinds is now legal in Indiana, as long as it's not on state soil, but in a boat floating above it!

Gee, I wonder who figured that one out?

Next thing you know, licenses are issued and huge multi-decked river gambling boats are now finding a home in selected small towns all along the Ohio river, from Ohio to Illinois.

These gambling boats, of course, are all moored to expensive land based facilities, which supply hotel and dinning accommodations, bars and live entertainment. Such a display of wealth that is staggering!

All the small town businesses are all for it in the beginning, hoping for a boost in business due to the volume of people that will be coming through their area to gamble at the boats.

All their hopes fade quickly though.

The boats are small cities within themselves. They provide everything and lack for nothing. The only thing gained by their existence there is the revenues paid to the towns and state, providing for bigger and better streets, highways and sewer systems, all of which benefit the boats too!

People flock to the boats to try their luck!

The state of Kentucky is now very unhappy. Their race tracks are losing money. Everyone is gambling on the boats now instead of playing the horses.

Kentucky vows to confiscate any gambling boat that ventures into what is considered to be Kentucky owned waters. It is a debatable invisible line at best.

So, the boats just venture a short distance from the dock and then return, not really going anywhere but just satisfying the legalities of their operation.

On the boat, a world like no other exists. People are drinking and smoking, creating a thick foggy cloud hanging in the

Life as I Lived It

air, while throwing fistfuls of money around, like there is no end to it. They mostly lose but win just enough to keep them coming back for more!

The casino has a huge marquis out on the highway, depicting scenes of people who have won $2,500, $4000, $5000, $12,000 or so and I can't help but wonder, how much did they spend to win only that amount?

Just think, you spend ten or twenty thousand dollars over a year or so time, just to be that five thousand dollar winner. Wow! Doesn't that make you so excited, you just want to rush right down there with your paycheck in hand and get right down to business, joining the action and trying your luck?

Well, you would be surprised how many people react in just that manner! Gambling can be just as addictive as any drug on the market!

Some people lose everything they own.

The gambling boat casino people do not intend for people to do that. That's bad publicity. It scares away players. I have known them to actually stop people from playing because they were getting in over their heads.

That is why there is a gamblers helpline that people who are addicted to gambling can call for help with their addiction.

A large majority of gamblers set a limit for themselves. They will spend $20, $50, or a $100 dollars and then quit.

Richard W. Block

If they win, then they play on the winnings or at least break even.

Then there's the high rollers deck. It's a whole area devoted to those who want to go broke quick or win big fast!

I watched a man put one hundred dollar bills into multiple slot machines as if they were only one dollar bills by most standards!

The old adage ran through my mind as I watched the machines devour his hundred dollar bills. "A fool and his money are soon parted." I would hate to think how many fools were there that day or there even now as I scribble this down, but you know what they say, "It's all in the cards!"

GETTING OLD

Getting old is such a depressing process. There are so many things that happen to the body as it ages that no one ever warns you about. I guess the older generation that have been there and done that, figure it's a private secret or something and that you will find out in good time for yourself. So, they say nothing.

Well, I don't know about you, but I like to be warned or at least informed about upcoming health problems before they sneak up on me.

For instance, my watch needed a new battery. I went to the jewelry counter at K-Mart where they sell the batteries and install them as well.

Usually I put the battery in myself, so I had already taken the old battery out and showed it to eh girl behind the counter. I told her that this was the battery I needed but I couldn't quite make out the model number on the back of it.

She said, "Oh, that's a number such and such, we have plenty of them in stock".

I said, "I guess you must sell a lot of that size and you recognized it at a glance."

She said, "No, I read the numbers on it. They're as plain as day, can't you read them?"

A few weeks later I was talking to a friend who was about my age. I noticed he had a pair of glasses in his shirt pocket. I said, "Gee Randy, I didn't know you wear glasses."

He said that he hadn't until recently. He had noticed that he was having trouble reading

fine print. I told him about my K-Mart experience with the watch battery and he said that's how it begins.

I said, "What do you mean?" He said, "Well I went to the eye doctor and spent hundreds of dollars on examinations and prescription eye glasses that I really didn't have to get. I found out from all of this, that at about 35 years of age, your eyes don't focus like they used to, due to the muscles in your eyes getting weaker with age. This changes for the worse about each five years age thereafter, requiring just a little stronger pair of glasses with each degree of change, which is normal as you get older. I could have gone to the drug store and bought a pair of reading glasses for five bucks if only someone would have told me!"

So that's what I eventually did, now that someone had given me that bit of information.

GHOSTS

Ghosts, now there is a topic that I don't feel to be in a class by itself. I think ghosts can be in the same class as U.F.O.'s.

Either you have seen them or you have not.

Either you believe in them or you do not.

In this world, most people agree that anything is possible.

I would say that most people believe in life after death. At least they are taught that through religion.

Well then, what is the big deal about believing in the existence of ghosts?

I grew up in a house built in 1810 along the Ohio river town of aurora. It was a three story house with two steep stairways connecting the floor levels.

We used the top floor for storage. It was kind of spooky up there because that is the stairway the man hung himself in!

Richard W. Block

I never knew his name but I am sure it is in the records somewhere if I really wanted to know.

It would stand to reason that if there was a ghost in the house, it would be him, but who knows how many people have died there in the almost two hundred years that have passed since the house was built or even before it was built.

My grandfather may have died there too. I have always assumed that he did.

What is a ghost anyway? Why does it exist? Is it a restless spirit that cannot find rest? Why does a ghost confine itself to a particular area? Ghosts usually seem to be a once living person of the past.

Sometimes they are seen very clearly and sometimes they are not, but their presence is made known by sounds or movement.

When I was seven or eight, I remember a rocking chair that used to sit in our living room in front of the T.V. At times, it would just start rocking back and forth all by itself with no one in it. It was a big heavy upholstered platform rocker. It was not a chair that a slight draft might cause it to move. Besides, you would feel a draft or breeze anyway and there was none! This happened frequently!

My mother used to remark, "well, I hope they (meaning he or she) likes the T.V. program we are watching. I would sure hate to make them mad!"

My mom was priceless at times with her witty comments.

Life as I Lived It

Mrs. Fauss, our elderly neighbor, always told my mother to ask the ghost who they were and what did they want when the chair was rocking, but mom would not do it.

She said she was afraid it might answer back!

Mrs. Fauss claimed that if those questions were asked the ghost would go away never to return.

Many years later, I found myself living in the old house alone. I had inherited it after my father passed on.

I used to hear all kinds of sounds, but they were not scary sounds like the proverbial chains rattling or moaning like the movies depict.

Every once in a while, I would see a wisp of smoke or small cloud of something like fog pass through my bedroom. It would come and go in seconds it seemed.

I used to bid it welcome and that the big old house was room enough for the both of us.

It never responded to me and I wasn't afraid of it. I suppose it knew that anyway. Besides, I found great comfort in the colt .45 automatic pistol I slept with beneath my pillow and I will tell you why

One morning I was sleeping in bed when I heard the door open downstairs. It is funny how light one sleeps when one is watching out for one's own rear end. I listened to the quiet sneaking footsteps coming up the stairs, coming closer and closer. Then a young man came through the doorway into my bedroom at the foot of my bed. He was holding a .38 revolver in his hand. He grinned and said, "now I've got ya".

You should have seen the look on his face when I flipped back the blanket and he was staring at the business end of my .45 auto! I grinned back and said, "I think my gun is bigger than yours!"

At that moment he said, "I think I am in the wrong house!" Then he turned and promptly left. I thought of Al Capone's immortal words, "a few kind words and a handgun go a lot further than a few kind words alone". Hell, I never doubted him!

Several times in Michigan at Mr. "G"'s house, several people experienced several happenings.

Several times late at night, a knocking on the bedroom door to Mr. G's bedroom would be heard. Each time the door was answered, no one was there. Several others saw a woman dressed in white with long dark hair. One second she was standing in their bedroom and then the next she was gone.

I awoke one night for some reason in the wee hours of the morning. As I opened my eyes, there she was! She was standing at the foot of my bed, looking out the window, white dress, dark hair and all! I starred a moment in disbelief. Then I closed my eyes and opened them to look again and she was gone in a blink.

Life as I Lived It

When I related what I had seen the next morning, everyone who had seen her before, confirmed my description as the same lady they had seen.

Mrs. G. was in poor health and when she eventually passed on, the lady ghost disappeared as well. Several of us wondered if there was a connection.

Maybe she wasn't a ghost at all, but a guardian angel instead.

You have heard the saying, "life is a mystery". Well, it truly is most of the time!

GRANDMA

"Doesn't it always seem to go that you don't know what you got till it's gone"?

(A phrase from the song "Big Yellow Taxi" by Joni Mitchell). How true it is though.

I was probably closer to my Grandmother than any other person in the world. She was born in the year 1900, so it was always easy to remember how old she was. I gave her a silver dollar dated 1900, mounted in a necklace, for her birthday once. She was proud of that simple little gift.

I learned a few things about cooking from her. I can still fry chicken just like hers and I make the best chicken gravy, second to none, thanks to her. She would make jelly from the blackberries I picked. She always poured paraffin on the top of the jelly in the open jelly jars to seal them.

I would bring home huge striped squash and pumpkins and we would sit on the front porch and peel and chunk them up to make pies of them. I haven't had a decent piece of squash pie since she passed on over forty years ago. You simply don't realize that when a person passes on all those

Life as I Lived It

recipes go with them. I should have paid more attention to her pie making.

When you are used to eating a person's cooking, no one else's will compare. It naturally just doesn't taste the same.

My Grandmother was born and raised on a farm and she was a hard worker. She told me her Father died when she was just a little girl He worked himself to death taking care of the family when they were all sick and couldn't do the chores. He died of pneumonia.

She loved animals and she always had a dog or a cat or a parakeet. Her little toy terrier, Buddy, was a lap dog. Every time you sat down he jumped up in your lap and was there to stay until you got tired of him and put him down.

My Dad's side of the family always raised beagle hounds for hunting and one day he brought home two beagle puppies. We kept them in a box in the kitchen where there was a hard floor and easy to clean up any mess they might make. Well, one day, one of the puppies ventured into the other room and pooped on the rug. I knew Grandma would be furious when she found out, so I said "Grandma Look what Buddy did!" I was right she grabbed up poor Buddy and rubbed his nose in it and then threw him outside in the back yard. I never dreamed she would do that. I felt so sorry for Buddy, running around, snorting, with that turd on his nose.

One freezing cold winter, I was running my trap line and I had caught a "woods" cat in one of my traps that I had set for raccoons. Well, you can't just let a wild cat out of a trap without them fighting and trying to tear you up. Experience had taught me to just shoot them and then remove them. I always carried a burlap sack to carry my traps and game in, so I just dumped the cat into the sack. When I got home, I remembered that I still had the cat in the sack. I had intended to get rid of it along the way home, but I forgot.

I pulled the cat out of the bag and it was frozen solid in an arched pose like cats do sometimes when a dog comes around. I stood him up against a clothesline pole and went into the house. After supper I looked out the door window and you could see the cat standing there life like. I pointed it out to Grandma and she said, "Oh, it must be hungry".

I thought I would get rid of it in the morning before I go to school, so she will think it just moved on to somewhere else.

While sitting in school, I remembered the cat! I Forgot! As soon as school was out I ran straight home. The cat was gone! I asked Grandma, "I wonder where that cat went, that was outside last night?" She said, "oh the poor thing. It was still there this morning, so I took it out a bowl of milk and it fell over dead. It must have frozen to death last night". Well what happened to the cat? She then said, "Well I wrapped it up in some newspapers. It wouldn't bend so I had to use some straight pins to hold the papers together. Then I put it in the garbage can". I went outside and removed the can lid and there it was, wrapped up like a big Christmas present. I never told her otherwise.

Grandma worked until the day she died. She was a paper hanger supreme. She would walk on a board suspended by

Life as I Lived It

two step ladders, putting wall paper on a ceiling. I think she had one heck of a sense of balance and direction to keep from falling off that board. I would sometimes help her. I would carry the ladders and the table, and then I would put the paste on the paper and fold it for her. She was an artist in her own rite. Paper hanging is one of those trades that have pretty much fallen by the wayside.

She had a 1963 Rambler car. It was a stick shift car. She wouldn't drive an automatic because you didn't shift the gears. It is funny how people are the opposite now days, most people can't drive a stick shift.

One of Grandma's sisters lived just down the street. Her name was Cornelia and she was married to Russell Welch. Uncle Russell had two big white horses in a stable that he rode in parades. My Cousin Jimmie and I would go down behind his stable where the manure pile was and dig fishing worms out of it occasionally. There were always red worms there. We also liked to visit the horses.

One day we went down to visit the horses and I noticed there was a bin full of ears of corn. I told Jimmie that I thought we should feed some corn to the horses. They looked hungry to me and it would be a treat for them, I thought.

Later on that afternoon, the phone rang and it was Uncle Russell and he wanted Jimmie and me to come see him. When we got there Uncle Russell asked us, "were you in the stable this morning?" We replied, "Yes". He asked, "Did you feed some corn to the horses?" We gave a shaky, "yes". We were getting the drift that maybe we had done something

Richard W. Block

pretty wrong by that time. Then Uncle Russell said, "Well, here's a nickel a piece for telling the truth". "Don't do it again!" Wow! A whole nickel a piece! Right to the candy store we went to get a big Three Musketeers candy bar. It's hard to believe that money was worth something back then.

Gas was twenty cents a gallon then too!!

GRANDPA'S FOOTSTEPS

I grew up in a small Indiana rural town on the banks of the Ohio River with its many creeks and backwaters. So, naturally hunting and fishing was a part of everyday life for many people just as it had been for many generations previous, being handed down from father to son many times over.

A heritage and simply a way of life would be a good explanation.

My Grandfather was a renowned rifle shot. His exploits and his rifle were legend. He had a Winchester model 70 in .220 swift caliber with a ten power Lymann target scope for long distance shooting. I'd heard many stories and saw many picture of my Grandfather with that rifle in hand.

I asked my Dad one day when I was about 12 years old, what ever happened to Grandpa's rifle. People would ask me about it from time to time and I had no idea what to tell them.

My Dad told me that when his Dad died, shortly after W.W. II ended, that he ended up with it, being the eldest son of the family. "Well, where did it go?" I asked. My Dad said that he sold it or got rid of it at the very least.

Now my Dad was a damn fine shooter and I couldn't understand why he would turn loose of a rifle like that. So I asked, "Why?" And I think it was at about that point in my life that my education of what absolute accuracy meant and what it took to achieve it.

My Dad said, "It was key holing so I got rid of it." And I sand "Key holing?" "What the heck is key holing?"

And Dad said, "Key holing is when a rifle starts throwing the bullet sideways. In other words, instead of the bullet hitting the target point first and leaving a round hole, it hits sideways leaving an oblong hole resembling a keyhole. When this starts happening, it means the barrel is shot out (the rifling is worn away) and it's not accurate anymore unless you replace the old barrel with a new one. You have to understand that the drawback of the .220 swift is that it is such a fast and hot shooting caliber that it shoots the barrel out!"

"Well how long does it take for that to happen?" I asked.

And Dad said, "Well, the way your Grandpa used to hand load his cartridges, a barrel was only good for about 200 shots because the bullet was traveling about 4500 feet per second, which is almost a mile in just a little over one second!"

I thought to myself that it's nice to have all of that power and speed but not at that price. If I ever build a varmint rifle of superior quality, the swift will not be a consideration.

Life as I Lived It

Years passed by all too quickly.

It's amazing how everybody knows everybody else and their entire relative in a small town community isn't it? Sometimes I think that's why people move to faraway places.

Well, anyway, I had been admiring a .222 caliber Browning Safari grade varmint rifle in a sporting goods store owned by an older gentlemen named Chick K, whom I had known forever it seems, because my relatives all bought their supplies from him I know that rifle had been sitting in his store for at least two years, because I had been looking at it almost every time I went there for something. I think it never sold because it had no sights on it. Besides, I think it was waiting for me. That $250.00 price tag was a lot of money in the mid 1960's.

So one day I said, "Chickadee", that's what I used to call the old fart, (lovingly of course) "I've made up my mind, and I want that Browning Rifle. I'll pay you what I can, whenever I can, if that's okay?"

Chick said, "Well I'll have to look around the back room because I'm not sure where the box for it is."

It was then for the first time in my life, that I realized that I had one hell of a credit line for a boy of 15 or 16 years old.

He meant for me to take that rifle with me for what few dollars I was putting down on it! When that fact hit me as he was handling me the rifle, I sand "no! no! no!" And Chick said, don't you want to take it with you?"

Richard W. Block

And again I said "no" you pout that rifle back in the rack and keep it for me. When I give you that last dollar that pays it off, then you can give it to me. I'll pay for it quicker if I don't have it to play with!" "Then we'll talk about that 10 power Unertel scope you have in the display case."

Needless to say, I paid for both in record time.

Somewhere in that time span my Dad passed on. So I had to find someone to give me sound advice.

That man was Buck Buchannan who was a champion trap shooter, expect rifle shot and reloader who owned a gun club in the neighboring town and had known my Dad and Grandfather. With Buck's guidance, I learned to float the barrel or bed the barrel. There are two different methods of making your rifle accurate.

By floating your barrel, you remove your barrel and action from the stock and remove enough wood from the stock where the barrel lies, so that when assembled, the barrel is touching nothing. The test is to take a dollar bill and slide it under the barrel between the stock and barrel, and slide it all the way down to the action without the bill touching anything but the barrel. If the dollar bill doesn't catch on anything the barrel is floating.

The purpose of floating is so the cold or heat of weather doesn't cause the stock and barrel to bind on each other causing poor accuracy.

Life as I Lived It

Bedding is putting a layer of fiberglass between the barrel and stock and pressing them together to form a bond between the two so there is no movement.

I like floating the best. I've taken average rifles and turned them into first rate head shooters on deer sized animals at 400 yards, when they could hardly make a body hit, before floating the barrel.

Needless to say, Buck advised me as well on reloading my own ammo that meets match grade specs. I, until then had not much faith in "reloads: until I learned that I could make better ammo than what the factory hands down!

And also, needless to say, I still have that rifle after 40 years and it has created many tall tales by many eye witnesses, some of them I'd find hard to believe myself if it wasn't for the photographs!

GROUND ZERO

I was at a function at the West Point Military Academy, which is up the Hudson River from New York and the 9-11 attacks on the Trade Center had happened previously. Two of my friends wanted to go to New York and see Ground Zero.

I asked them, "How were they going to get there?" And Brett said they were going in Jeff's pick-up truck. I laughed and said, "No you aren't". They asked why not and I told them they wouldn't even get close driving a vehicle and if they did make it, there would be no place to park.

"How would you go?" they asked. I said, "I would go across the river to the train station and take the train into Grand Central Station by Times Square and then take the Subway to Ground Zero." Then they said to come with them and be their guide. I really needed to be at the Point, but I was able to get away for a while, so off we went to New York on the train.

I warned them that we will be walking down the street among thousands of people who all look like Americans until they open their mouth and no English comes out. I

Life as I Lived It

told them they would be lucky to find someone that speaks English!

We switch from the train to the subway and got off a block away from Ground Zero. When we came up to the street from the subway, we saw hundreds of people in a line waiting to see the ruins at the end of the block, facing where the twin towers once were.

There was a large plywood wall leading to a large viewing platform, overlooking the site. The wall divided the people coming and going to and from the platform.

There was a New York police woman standing in the middle of everything, answering people's questions. I heard her tell someone that you have to have a ticket to be able to get in line to see the site and the ticket place was three blocks down the street, but there were no more tickets for today.

We went up to her and got the same story. We were in uniform and I told her we only had a few hours and we had to be back to the Point. She looked around and slipped us three tickets from her tunic and said, "Don't tell anyone where you got these, now go get in line."

We thanked her and got in line.

There was a church on the corner with a small graveyard behind it. You had to pass by it as you moved toward the viewing platform. There was a blanket of thick gray ash caked on all the gravestones and covered the ground as well as the church itself. I bet there was grass buried under the ash, but there was nothing showing to indicate it.

They would let twenty five people at a time for a period of five minutes to see and take pictures on the platform. Then you had to move on for the next group to come up.

Things were moving along pretty well. There were two young girls in front of us in the line and one of them had red hair and freckles, so I thought I'd strike up a conversation while we were waiting our turn. I asked her where she got those freckles and she turned and gave me this look like who the heck are you? She said nothing and turned back to her girlfriend and resumed their conversation.

I then said, "I bet you got them from your Mother." Again, the same result. I remembered telling Brett and Jeff earlier about people not speaking English, so I listened in on their conversation and they were speaking French. I said, "Quebec eh?" And she said, "No France." I said, "parley voux English?" And she gestured a tiny bit with two fingers.

When we made it on the viewing platform, we could barely get up front, there were so many people squeezing in to see the giant hole that was still being cleaned up and put into dump trucks and hauled away. It must have been ten stories deep.

It was awesomely huge. We let the two French girls in front of us so they could take their pictures. I'd seen enough and went down the exit ramp to the end of the walk.

Life as I Lived It

There was a man with a table full of religious materials and he asked me if I was a Christian?

I saw English and Spanish printed materials and I thought, oh crap, I don't want to get into a conversation, so I answered, "Bitte?" which is please? In German. I said that I didn't understand in German, to kill the conversation, because Brett and Jeff would be here any minute to leave. The man said, "Oh! German! I have some pamphlets in German somewhere here in a box under the table." The guys showed up as he was searching and we left pretty quickly.

We hopped on the subway and we were trying to figure out our way back. A Hispanic lady with her son, seated across from us, gave us a map to use. She spoke no English either.

As my Nephew Jim always says, "We were making memories."

GROWING UP

Do you ever worry about your children? Am I raising them right? Are other people having a good or bad influence on them? Are they smoking or drinking or into drugs when they are elsewhere with friends of theirs? What can make things right?

I'm not a big drinker. I don't smoke nor am I into drugs.

My parents drank and smoked and heaven knows they gave me all the opportunities to do the same, but I don't.

Why is that? What made the difference? I'll tell you about my parents and how I was raised and how I did the same for my own children.

When I was a baby and was big enough to drink from a glass, my parents gave me beer to drink. Beer? They gave beer to a baby? Oh Yes!!

We used to have these shot glasses that were shaped like miniature beer mugs. That was my portion, a shot glass of beer. Sure, my parents got criticized from their friends, so what our family was of German Heritage and the heritage

Life as I Lived It

of Germans is to drink beer! Just like it's the heritage of the French to drink wine and so on.

Even though our German ancestors were long gone, beer was still a part of family life. I never saw my Dad or Mom Drunk. I can say that I never saw them even a little tipsy, nor any of my Aunts and Uncles either.

Everyone knew their limit and quit when they reached it. It's just something you learn as you go through life.

Of course, when I was a teenager I just had to get drunk and make a fool of myself and then get sick, just to find out what it was like. This helped me establish my limit real quick.

I think the part about making a fool out of myself, especially in front of girls, hurt me the worse then the sick part.

My Dad used to tell me all the time, "if you want to drink beer, get one out of the fridge and drink it here. You don't have to run around with your friends to drink beer, you can have all you want right here at home. If your friends want a drink, invite them over. You don't have to run around to drink beer."

It was that common sense gesture that made running around and drinking beer with my buddies "No big deal".

When you are raised with something as an everyday part of life, it is "No big deal".

Richard W. Block

When you are told something is no good for you or it is wrong or bad, it only creates a mystery to be more eagerly explored by you so you can see for yourself.

I think parents cause their children to drink and smoke more often than not by telling their children no, rather than showing them for certain.

Here are some examples from my family.

I remember when I was about six year old and we were at one of my Dad's friends home on a Saturday night where they usually got together and played cards all evening.

My Dad was lighting up a cigarette and I said, "Gee that looks like something good, can I have one?" My Dad said, "Sure, and stuck a cigarette in my mouth. He lit it up with his ever present Zippo lighter saying, "here, and suck that in now." Of course I coughed my ass off as he expected I would do and said, "Now isn't that good?" Of course I coughed out a No! Answer. "Well then don't do it," Dad said. I then said "'Well if it's no good, then why do you smoke?"

Dad then said, "It's because I don't know any better, but you do, so don't smoke. It is just that simple."

My Uncle Ed James used to chew tobacco and he was shoving a wad into his mouth one day as he sat on the top step of the front porch when I was curious enough to say, "Hey, let me try some of that Uncle Ed!" Uncle Ed said, "Sure, here you go boy," as he shoved a wad of tobacco into my mouth. "Now just chew on that and don't swallow any.

Life as I Lived It

Just keep it in your jaw and spit once in a while when you need to. That's some good stuff ain't it?"

In no time flat I was spitting that crap out and turning green. I was sick for two days. Guess what? I never had any desire to chew tobacco either!

A lot of people would think this to be terrible, but a lot more probably wish someone would have done these things to them before they got into the bad habits they are now trying to kick!!!

HALLOWEEN

I was listening to a radio program the other day and the D.J. s were talking about apples and whether children liked eating them as much now days as they did when they were kids. One remarked that he used to get an occasional apple during Trick or Treat and how he would have rather had candy instead.

I remember getting an apple or two and I didn't mind them as long as they were not too ripe. I like apples when they are hard and juicy and a bit on the sour side of ripe. I remember keeping my bag held high enough that the apple didn't have enough drop distance to go through the bottom of my bag! We used paper bags in those days.

Living in a small town, most of the homes had outhouses (outside toilets) and one of the Halloween traditions was to tip the outhouses over on its side for a prank. Occasionally there would be someone in one and that would cause a hilarious ruckus.

A friend of mine used to put on an oversized pair of coveralls and stuff them full of newspapers to fill them the rest of the way out, kind of like a huge poppin fresh

Life as I Lived It

doughboy with a mask on and then sit on his porch like a big dummy decoration, waiting for the Trick or Treaters to show up. Of course he would sit there motionless while the kids were waiting for someone to come to the door for their treats.

Sometimes they would talk to each other wondering if the dummy was real and a lot of times they would poke or kick the big dummy to see if it would move, but Frank would just play dead until the kids got their candy and were ready to leave. That is when Frank would rise up while screaming and growling and chase the Trick or Treaters while they were screaming bloody murder and scattering into the night's darkness! He should have videotaped that prank, but that was before video cameras existed.

Squirt guns, water balloons and water hoses were other fun tools as well. I will let your imagination or memories be your guide on those things.

Then, there were the people that gave out money instead of candy. That was always a challenge. They would come to the door wearing oven mittens, holding a cookie sheet with various size coins on it and you could have whatever you wanted on the tray as long as you could pick some up and hang on to them. The catch was that they just pulled the tray out of the oven and those coins were too hot to even try to pick one up! Needless to say, there were still most of the coins still on the sheet at evening's end.

My son Bubba (the raccoon) loved Halloween. He liked greeting the kids at the door and looking at all the different costumes. But even better, he liked going through their bags of candy, if he could get hold of them, and picking out what he wanted. The kids were always mesmerized by the sight of him and they were lucky to get away with more candy than they came with!

Halloween has changed a lot with all the new decorations people place on and in their homes. Lighted blow up figures, orange lights and grave stones in their yards, but the kids are still kids no matter how old they are!!

In the rural towns and neighborhoods, the adults went along with the kids as well. The difference is that the adults did their Trick or treating with a shot glass in hand. While the kids were getting their candy, the adults were getting shots of booze. If it weren't for the pictures, they would not have known how great a time they had Trick or Treating!

HANDGUN CARRY PERMITS

The proposed Ohio handgun permit system. What is it really about?

There is a lot of misconception and negativity about it because it has never been explained properly, so I will try to set the record straight.

There is a misunderstanding that if Ohio adopts a permit system, everyone will be walking around with a "pistol in their pocket." It will be like the old west, I have heard said.

This is as far from the truth as one can get. The purpose of the handgun permit system in Ohio is to be recognized by the other forty some odd states as an equal, which already have permit systems.

As it stands now, an Ohio resident cannot take a handgun into any other state for any purpose without it being confiscated and the owner prosecuted. Why? Because Ohio does not have a permit system! Even if an Ohio hunter possess a valid non-resident hunting license, which specifies a handgun can be used for hunting purposes, his handgun will be confiscated because a valid handgun permit is also required, even though it is not indicated on the hunting license. Thus the state of Ohio is not recognized by other states as an equal!

Ohio needs to institute a permit system and the sooner the better.

Sure, a concealed handgun permit is part of the program, but the stringent requirements to obtain a concealed carry permit, insures that only those who qualify will be the only persons carrying a concealed handgun and these numbers will be small as compared to the number of people obtaining hunting and target practice permits.

This gives the Ohio law enforcement community a very good grasp on who is able to possess and use handguns in the state of Ohio.

This is a very good step in the right direction. If it does come to pass, a lot of their problems will be solved and barriers broken.

GOOD GOING OHIO!!

HOLSTERS

I've written about hunting and using handguns and target shooting and so on but I haven't really gotten into the subject of holster.

It used to be that no matter what kind of holster you used, it was generally made of leather and so was the belt you used with it.

I used to have all kinds of belts and holsters made of leather and I hated them all! Why?

Because it's the nature of leather to make a creaking noise every time you have it on!

I used to hate to pass a cop on foot. The creaking sound of his leather equipment would get where he was going long before he would.

Can you imagine trying to hunt with a leather rig on in the woods, on a calm day? Every time you made a movement, it would sound like someone opening a creaky screen door.

Of course, you can rub it down with saddle soap or neat's-foot oil and this would quiet things down for a while, but not entirely.

I always preferred Mexican leather over American. The Mexicans use a different process to tan their leather. I don't know what they do so different from the Americans, but I do know that Mexican leather will not turn your cartridges green from mold like American leather does when you have them in the provided shell loops of the belt. Mexican leather is also lined so it doesn't creak but very little as well.

In spite of it all, I was really glad to see the advent of nylon holsters come to being. I think the Uncle Mike's brand name was one of the fore runners of the market. I have many of their holsters and favor their line of products because of the quality in material and craftsmanship and design as well. And, of course, they are silent to carry, because they are nylon, a silent material. Nylon holsters are also easier on your guns because they don't wear the blue finish off your weapons like leather does.

I have just about every manner of holster as I'm sure you can imagine. Holsters are like golf clubs. You have different ones for different applications.

When I'm hunting, I like to use a left handed holster, even though I'm right handed. I slide the holster around behind me in the middle of my back so I can access it easily with my right hand.

Life as I Lived It

The advantages of this are many, some being, it can't snag on the underbrush, tree limbs,

saplings, etc. Any noise it makes is behind you, blocked by your body and it's easy to reach.

So, chances are, you won't see me wearing one, unless I turn my back.

If I'm using a right hand holster, I usually wear it on my left side in front. This is called a cross-draw because you are reaching across your body to draw your weapon. This type of carry is very comfortable and it allows easy access in a sitting position, especially in a vehicle.

Look at a policeman's duty belt sometime. You'll notice that the police carry their side arms on their sides in holsters that sit high on their belts. This is supposed to let the officer sit down with his rig on.

I'd think you'd just about have to be double jointed to be able to get your handgun out of a rig like that while sitting in a vehicle.

A holster set up that I use all the time for concealed carry and not for hunting, is a rig called the belly band. It comes in two colors, black and flesh color. I like the flesh color because it more resembles a medical support brace as opposed to a holster set up. It's a five inch or so, wide, strips of elastic, with Velcro on each end that wraps tight around your chest like a back brace. It has pockets all around it and can hold two handguns, one under each arm if you like, leaving no discernable bulges to give away their hiding place.

This is not a quick access rig, because you have to unbutton your shirt first to reach your gun or guns. Because of this, most people don't suspect anyone to be carrying handguns in this hard to reach manner. So this deters suspicion that you may be armed at a glance. This is a plus! This is in your favor!

If you're worried about survival in the city and it's known that you carry a gun, carry two instead of one. Carry the first one in an obvious, easily found position, unloaded. Carry the second one loaded and well hidden. If the obvious one is wrestled from you and the fool who has it things you're at his mercy, boy is he in for a big surprise!

Just remember this, choose your holsters to fit your tactics and the best tactic of all is to steer clear of trouble!

HOLY SMOKE

When I was a lad of 7 or 8 my neighbor's daughter was getting married. My sister Mary Jane, 2 years younger, was to be the flower girl.

We lived in an old neighborhood in a small river town and most of my neighbors ere retired folks, there being few kids of course.

There was a small German Church around the corner at the beginning of our street overlooking the Ohio River. It had the big oak hardwood benches lining the aisle way which ran down the center of the church.

I was sitting with my Grandmother on the edge of the main aisle about half way. The piano was playing "Here comes the Bride" as my sister lead the procession tossing the rose petals from her little basket.

All of a sudden, a horrible urge from within hit me. There was no holding back. I tilted and let go. The sound reverberated off the oak bench like a magnified megaphone; they even heard it down the street. The music stopped. Everyone was looking around and at each other with the "who did that?" look on their face. I, disbelieving and in shock, started laughing. It was at the point that my Grandmother started hitting me with a vengeance, using her purse with the long loop handles that all the old folks carry "letting the cat out of the bag", as to who the guilty person was.

HOLY SMOKE!!!

HOOSIER HOSPITALITY

Once upon a time in the mid 1970's, I was dating a young lady who was a college student at Thomas Moore College in Kentucky.

I lived in Aurora, a small rural town along the Ohio River in Indiana.

I guess she must have invited some of her college friends for a visit, because one Saturday afternoon, a boy and girl couple presented themselves at the door looking for my girlfriend.

Their names were Tim and Tina and they belonged to the same poet/writer group as my girlfriend did at college.

It was obvious that they thought themselves to be intellectual of some degree with their proper mannerism and speech and Tim's well groomed beard and his smoking pipe.

Boy! What a pair of city slickers, I thought to myself.

I will just have to roll out the red carpet and show them some of that good old Hoosier Hospitality!

So, we sat around and "chewed the fat", so to say, well into the afternoon.

"You must stay for dinner", I proclaimed. I told them we were having fried chicken and fresh corn on the cob. Yum! Yum!

I slid out the back door and headed for the neighboring farmers corn field, where I knew the corn was ripe for picking.

A dozen ears of corn later I was back in the kitchen husking the corn as my girlfriend put the skillet on with the two squirrels and young ground hog that I had shot the day before.

I told her distinguished friends that she had never cut up a whole chicken before and that is why the pieces looked funny.

Soon, dinner was served and Tim and Tina were going through that "chicken" like a buzz saw.

After each had a sizable pile of bones on their plates, I asked them, "How did they like the chicken?" "It is great", they replied.

So I said, "well, I am going to have to level with you, it is not really chicken."

Life as I Lived It

Tim said, "I have been trying to determine which parts of the chicken I have eaten, but the bones just don't look like they should".

I said, "Well, that is because it is squirrel and ground hog".

Almost instantly, the pieces of meat they were holding in their fingers dropped onto their plates with a clinking sound and with eyes the size of silver dollars, they were asking in unison, "what have I eaten so far? Have I eaten any of the ground hog?"

I looked through their piles of bones and declared that they had only eaten squirrel so far. And that was the last time I ever saw Tim and Tina.

I have often wondered as I think back to that meal, what ever became of them and if that had any kind of bearing on their future lifestyle.

It is like anything else. For them I cannot say, but for me, it sure made my day!!

HOW I BUILT MY HOUSE

In the early 190's I bought my farm from a bank that had foreclosed on the property and was selling it at a bargain price because no one wanted it. The place was in a terrible run down condition. People had been driving their off road vehicles up and down the hilly roads, causing erosion so bad that you couldn't even walk on them. It took a bulldozer a solid eight hours of dozing, just to make the roads passable and tons and tons of creek rock to provide a base to be able to drive a truck on.

There was junk cars and trash everywhere that had to be hauled away.

The house on the property, sat on a shelf in the middle of a hillside. It was not visible from the main road because it was also in woods. The house was in worse condition than the roads. All of the windows were broken out and the roof leaked. The rains and winds blew through destroying he wall panels and flooring. It was a one story, flat roofed, concrete block house, built on a slab of concrete. The exterior had spray painted graphitic all over it. What a mess.

Life as I Lived It

The bank I bought the place from was a very friendly, small town bank and they were more than happy to set me up with a construction loan, being I did them a great service by taking the place off their hands.

A construction loan is a type of loan that gives you money as you need it with a time limit of three months to complete your project, before you have to start paying it back. There is no interest put on the money used until the three months are reached.

I was in the middle of a divorce at that time and I had no money and no place to stay.

At one of the hearings, the Judge said, "How can you build a house in the middle of this divorce?" I said, "I'm tired of living in my car!"

I did everything I could to save money on materials. I went to construction sites and got scrap materials. I went to lumber companies and bought bundles of 2x4 studs from the railroad cars as it was unloaded.

I stripped out houses that were being torn down and got wiring and light fixtures. Anything I could use, I stored away. I had so much stuff accumulated that I only used some of it and had stuff left over. I went to tile companies and bought left over or discontinued tile by the pallet at giveaway prices.

I hired three men to help. Two of them always worked together and the other was a loner, but I knew them all and how good their work ethics were, so I had a lot of confidence in them.

At the time, ten dollars an hour was a fair wage, so that is what we agreed on.

We drew up plans to make the house 2 stories tall, using the existing first story as the foundation to build on. We stripped out and moved existing walls to make the bathroom much bigger and a utility room out of the remaining space, instead of a bedroom.

We insulated all of the interior as well as the exterior walls. I did this so I could use and heat as much or as little of the house by simply closing doors. Each room had its own electric heat with a wall thermostat.

The house had a fireplace, so I found some bricks for free and extended the chimney above the roofline to get a good draft. I bought a fireplace insert out of the newspaper ads and installed it in the fireplace. It had a built in blower. That worked out really nice.

At one point I started to get phone calls from my guys. They couldn't see eye to eye on how to build some parts of the house, so I gathered the three of them together for a talk.

I told them that I chose them to build my house because of their different talents and I knew some of them would be over lapping and I knew they had different ways of doing the same task or project.

Life as I Lived It

I told them that the goal here was to build me a house. I don't care if it is built the fast way, the slow way, the cheap way or the costly way, I just want it the best way to last a life time and as maintenance free as can be possible. Just get together if you have a problem and decide which the best way is, then make it happen!

After that, there were no more phone calls. They worked together like a finely turned machine. Even after my house was finished, they would get together and work other jobs.

I tiled the entire ground floor with the tile I bought.

Every room was wired for a telephone. A friend of mine who worked for the phone company did that for me at no charge. It's great to have friends that will do those kinds of things for you.

The guys had a texture sprayer. They mixed the paint and plaster together and sprayed all the walls and ceilings in one day.

I bought rough cut cedar boards and did all the baseboards, door and window frames with it.

I made a pantry under the staircase that leads up to the second floor loft where the three bedrooms are. I also built a safe room that has a secret book shelf door for access.

I designed and built my own water system for the well. My neighbor worked for Bobcat and he borrowed a trencher from work to lay the water lines to the house. He brought the trencher in the back of his small pickup truck and began to show me how to use it. I said, "Why don't you unload it first?" He said that it was okay and there would be no problem with where it was. So he started it up and began to show me what each lever does and that's when the trencher ate right through the cab of his truck before he could get it stopped.

I had to laugh after the shock was over. I had warned him, but he insisted. It was funny anyway.

I bought all my roof shingles from a place in a small town that dealt in seconds. The shingles I bought didn't have enough dark flecks in their color, but they all matched each other, so what!

I bought enough shingles to do the house and pole barn for a fraction of the price and they were still warranted for 25 years.

I had a budget of thirty five thousand dollars when I took out the construction loan and I used it all up. When the house was finished, it was worth seventy five thousand and that was in the early 1990's.

Most of the time now days when you build a house, the rule of thumb is fifty percent of the cost is materials and the other fifty is labor.

I DROWNED

I drowned when I was about 6 years old.

My parents and Aunts and Uncles and cousins would all get together and have family outings. We had weekend campouts, fishing, picnics and swimming all along different creeks in different backwoods areas.

One weekend we were having a family gathering and picnic at one of the swimming holes on Hogan Creek. Among the relatives were my three cousins, Mike, Eddie and George and we were all in the swimming hole having a good time and cooling off.

I couldn't swim, so I was floating around in a tire inner tube minding my own business when from beneath me up came my cousin Eddie, whom I believe was part fish when it came to water play. Needless to say, the inner tube flipped over, sending me to the bottom of the creek.

To this very day, I can still see the mud and rocks of the creek bottom as I lay there on my stomach. The air bubbles streaming from my nose and mouth, going upward to

Richard W. Block

somewhere. I couldn't move, I was to frozen somehow, is the only way I can describe myself.

All of a sudden I felt a hand grab me under one of my armpits and pull me up out of the watery grave and shake the water out of me. The next thing I knew, I was on the creek bank, gaging and gasping for air. It was my cousins' Dad, Dick, who had luckily pulled me up and had been keeping a close eye on us boys in the water.

As a result, I was terrified of going in the water. I never went swimming again until I was a teenager in the Boy Scouts. They tried to teach me every year at summer camp to swim, but I just couldn't bring myself to get in the lake and try. I would sit on the lake shore and watch all the other boys swim and observe how each boy swam. I found I could learn a lot of things by watching other people, but I still stayed away from the water.

Once a year, the Boy Scout District would get to use the Greendale swimming pool. Lots of scouts from different troops would spend the evening passing tests and learning different things in the water.

My Scoutmaster of several years had just about had it with me and my fear of water. I really didn't mind swimming pools because you knew and could see how deep the water was that you were in.

The straw that broke the camel's back, as to say, was when Buck explained and showed me that it was impossible to sink and stay down if your lungs were full of air. You always come to the surface and bob around. He showed me

Life as I Lived It

a thing called the jelly fish float and made me do it. It was true. You cannot sink when you are full of air.

Buck knew I definitely didn't like putting my head in the water, so he taught me the breast stroke. Before long, I was doing all the strokes. I really liked the back stroke I could make some distance with that one and it didn't tire me out.

I knew I had to swim and swim pretty well to pass the requirements to make Eagle rank.

My friend Marty H. helped me a lot. We were the same age and Marty seemed to be part fish in the water. There wasn't anything he couldn't do in the water.

As the years passed and I traveled around, I developed a love for snorkeling in the ocean. It is a different kind of water and you can float easier in salt water than in fresh water. I could go to sleep in the ocean while snorkeling very easily without trying too hard.

Buck, my Scoutmaster and Marty my Eagle brother have passed on by many years. People like these are never really gone, as long as they are remembered often. Remember that. You will find it to be all too true, no matter whom.

They are called Memories.

ISLAND LIFE, BAHAMAS

When my boss sold his franchise of 42 Mcdonalds restaurants back to the Mcdonalds Corporation in Oak Brook, a Chicago suburb, the management employees were paid their pension and profit sharing monies, to do with as they pleased.

The majority rolled their funds over into an IRA program for their eventual retirement. I rolled over half of mine and kept the other half to use for various things.

One of the things I invested in was a Time Share in the Bahamas. It was call Abaco Townes by the Sea and it was on Abaco Island.

The Bahamas are made up of several islands. Nassau is the largest. It has the main hospital facilities and is the largest city with all the gambling casinos and crime to boot!

Freeport is the next largest and is like a small town type island with a casino as well and little crime.

Abaco Island is a 100 mile long island that's one mile wide with Marsh Harbor in the center. It has no casinos and

Life as I Lived It

zero crime. There is a police force of only 12 officers for the whole island. It's a country or rural environment. The people are very friendly and very religious. There is a liquor store next to each church.

If you buy a beer, the cashier will open it for you automatically unless you tell them you are not going to drink it now or you are on your way home. Yes, drinking and driving is perfectly legal there. Why? Because the people do not abuse their privileges like we do here. So, there is no law against it.

When someone goes into town in a pickup truck, it is common to see the truck bed full of people standing in it coming through town. It is ok, you don't have to wear a seat belt if you don't speed and obey the law. You never see someone speeding or drunk or belligerent. No arguments or even a raised voice. Everyone greets you on the streets. It is just a great environment because there is no prejudice or racism there.

Our time share was a cottage on the shore with a small beach.

Telephones are not used too much. Everyone uses marine radios. All the bars and stores have marine radio set on channel 16. If you want to order a pizza, they are on channel 14. If you want a taxi or to talk to the ferry to see when it is coming in or going out, you just go to their channel and call them. I always took a marine radio with me when I was there.

Richard W. Block

A great thing about the Bahamas is that there are NO taxes! No sales tax, no income taxes, no property tax, no tax for anything! If you make a dollar, you get the whole dollar. Isn't that great!

How does the government get money, you may wonder? Import duties. Materials or good coming into the islands have to pay import duties and some of the duties are pretty stiff. If you buy a new car and bring it in, you have to pay one half of the buying price for the duty. If you buy another new car within three years, the duty is waived. If there is a disaster like a hurricane, they will waive the duties on replacement materials for a limited time.

People are allowed to go to the U.S.A. and do their shopping and are allowed a duty free limit of six hundred dollars per year. Most people wait until Christmas time to go.

The Bahamas don't actually have a Christmas. They have Junkanew. It lasts for two weeks to the end of the year. It's very much like our New Orleans Mardi Grau, with the parades and costumes and music.

There's always music playing all year round. You go shopping in a grocery store and you get so used to the beat of their music that you find yourself dancing down the aisles, unaware that you are even doing it. All their music has that same rhythm, even the Christmas music! You don't even know it's Christmas music unless you listen to the words.

The Bahamians are forbidden to gamble. It's a law. The government does not want its people to waste their money gambling. It can be better spent on their family's welfare.

Life as I Lived It

They have fee medical provided by the government. The doctors' fees are set by the government so there is no competition.

The daily routine of most of the people is to get into their boat each morning and go fishing. Around noon they come in to the docks and clean their catch on the provided tables. The fishermen have two buckets. Part of the catch goes into one bucket for his family use and the rest goes in the other bucket, which is sold to a restaurant or fish market.

The money is spent on beer and gas for the boat and then they are gone again to do the same thing in the evening, six days a week. Sunday is the day of rest and worship.

As you tour around the islands you will see a lot of homes in different stages of being built. The people do not borrow money to build a house. It takes them years most of the time.

They will buy some materials from time to time when they can afford them and work on the house when they can.

If you or I wanted to buy some property there, it might take years. They have to search the property titles back a couple hundred years to be sure it can be sold to you. Then there's the high cost of materials and the duties, unless you wait for the next hurricane. A wood frame house doesn't work; it needs to be concrete and steel to hold up in storms. It's against the law to bring in outside help. You have to use local labor or you can build it yourself and use relatives of yours if they have skills.

Richard W. Block

The down side of my Time Share was when there was storm damage to the condos, all the timeshare holders had to chip in their share of repair costs plus a yearly maintenance fee.

We used to go the beginning of December each year and I miss the always blowing breeze and the salt water air. I used to lie in bed and listen to the waves hitting the shore and the palm trees rustling in the breeze.

I used to carry a machete with me on the airplane. I was only questioned one time when my bag went through the x-ray machine. The attendant asked me if I had a really large knife in my bag and I told him, "Yes". He asked me what I needed that for and I told him it was a machete and I used it to whack open coconuts. He said, "Okay".

That was before the 9-11 crises of course. I couldn't get away with that now.

On a Thursday or Friday the people staying in the condos would have a giant block party. The purpose was to eat up all the food that you didn't want to take home with you. I always knew where I could pick fresh fruit from trees and coconuts that were ripe for eating, so I'd bring those things. There was no end to meeting and making new friends.

I always thought I'd like to live there, if they would have me.

JAMAICA

It was raining hard; the Jamaican airliner was pitching back and forth in the darkness and down pour. The visibility was almost zero. Somewhere down there is Montego Bay. The plane kept speeding up and slowing down as if it was searching for something. The runway I am thinking.

The pilot is searching for the runway. Surely, he knows where it is. With all the instrumentation he can't help but know. The plane was descending. The passengers were very restless to say the least. We could see Montego Bay below through the Torrance of wind and rain that was pounding the windows.

Everyone was holding their breath. It looked as though we were landing in the water. The runway lay right beside the bay and in fact covered with inches of water almost blending in with the bay.

A sigh of relief swept through the entire plane as it taxied to a stop. Everyone spontaneously began clapping and cheering.

"Please remain seated", was the response of the pilot through the speakers. "We will not be disembarking for a while, due to the weather conditions".

So we just sat there, most of us anyway. There are always those, who are in such a big hurry, who didn't sit, but stood there in the isle with their baggage at hand the entire time!

After an hour wait and not being able to withstand the grumbling any longer, the pilot announced that anyone who wanted to disembark could do so at their own risk.

The door was then opened and people began to descend the mobile stairway down to the water covered asphalt runway and running with splashing leaps to the terminal doorway.

After the mad rush for the terminal had subsided, I was able to retrieve our carryon bags from the overhead compartment in preparation for our exit. It looked like there would be no end to the storm very soon so I just told myself, "What the heck, I am going to get wet anyway, so I might as well get off the plane right now", so I did.

As I walked down those stairs to the tarmac, I had an experience like none I have ever had in my life. It was raining hard, but I felt I wasn't getting wet. I stood at the foot of the steps and motioned my wife to come on down. I yelled, "Come on! Don't worry, you won't get wet."

She didn't believe me of course, until she came down the steps and stood with me in the rain! We just stood there in the down pour, but it had no effect on us.

Life as I Lived It

The temperature of the rain drops must have been 98.6 F, because you could not feel it on you. When it rains back home in Indiana, the drops are cold, even in the summer and they make you hurry to find shelter.

Not so in Jamaica Monn. It was amazing. We took our time and strolled to the terminal in no hurry.

Once inside the airport terminal, we were shocked. Water was running out the doors as we came in! The roof leaked everywhere. Water was dripping from above, as well as running down the walls and hallways. What a mess. They didn't seem to be concerned about it. I figured it must just be their way of life. I was more right than I realized at the time.

We checked our baggage through customs with no problems.

It's amazing. The respect you get when you display an American passport is incredible. The little blue book with the American eagle crest on the cover says it all! All doors open, all barriers disappear it's a great feeling.

I asked at customs if American money was accepted there, or was it better to exchange it for Jamaican money. They advised me to exchange it and spend the local money so I would not have to worry about getting fair exchange rates if I used American dollars.

They had a convenient exchange window right there at the end of the pass through. I walked up to the window and asked the exchange rate for U.S. dollars. He said "forty".

I am thinking, "That is pretty good. Canada is $1.25 so $1.40 is better!"

If figured we would probably spend a couple hundred dollars easy, during our week stay, so I gave the clerk two one hundred dollar bills and said. "Exchange this into local money for me please."

He took the money and said, "Well, let's see that will be eight thousand Jamaican dollars as he counted out this huge stack of colorful bank notes."

I said, in shock, "What did you say the exchange rate is?" He said, "Forty that is forty Jamaican dollars for each American dollar." I said, "Damn, I think I am going to need a bag to carry that in!"

I showed my wife the big wad of cash and wondered if the bank back home would be stupid enough to apply this to my mortgage at face value?

No, I don't think so either, but it would be a fun gag to try!

We grabbed our bags and went outside beneath a long awning to the taxi area, where transportation was supposed to be waiting to take us to our condo complex in Negril, a hundred miles away.

We were over an hour late because of the storm. I was relieved to find the young man and his wife, who were to pick us up, were till there waiting for us to finally arrive. I don't know who among us was happiest to see each other.

Life as I Lived It

The luggage barely fit in the back of their little Toyota wagon, but we were loaded and on our way.

The rain persisted with a vengeance. I don't know which was worse, the roads or the visibility. I hate countries where you drive on the left side of the road and this was one of them, with one exception, you drove on the good parts of the road, regardless of which side the good parts were on and dodge to the left when you met another car coming at you.

Our driver seemed to know every pothole and dodged them like some kind of obstacle course. There weren't many lights along the way because there is not much electric. Most islands have huge diesel power plants to generate electric for those who can afford it. It is expensive and Jamaica was no exception

Our route was over the mountains, keeping to the high ground, because the coast roads were under water in places due to the storm.

We passed people all along the way, just standing there in the rain, doing nothing, not going anywhere, just standing there! And this is at two O'clock in the morning in the pitch black of the night.

I later learned that a lot of these people just simply have nothing to do but stand around doing exactly that, nothing.

Finally, we arrived at our condo complex where we were to spend the week. It was a typical operation. We were on the ground floor just a stone throw from the ocean beach. They had a large Jacuzzi next to the swimming pool and club house bar, which also had a large covered patio with plenty of tables and chairs for dining. They served meals there every day. You could pay by the meal or buy a week long meal package. You could enjoy a cool ocean breeze while eating and watching the activities on the beach…This is also where the condo complex held its weekly meetings, where everyone was welcomed and the ground rules were laid out. Then they would have some of the local business affiliates, introduce themselves and show everyone what they had to offer in the way of tours, fishing, hiking, boating, diving, snorkeling and rentals.

When that was done, you could sign up for whatever interested you and plan your week.

We were informed at the meeting that you would be approached on the beach by people selling marijuana from time to time, and if that is something you like to use, go ahead and buy all you want. "Take it back to your room and burn the house down!" was the manager words. "We only ask that you don't drive or leave the grounds while smoking pot. It is illegal here but the police are bribed, so you won't have any problems if you stay close."

He also, stated that it is perfectly ok for the girls to go topless. He then said, "We do prefer for you to wear a bottom even though it is not a law".

It was strange at first, walking down the mile and a half of beach, seeing all those girls toasting their titties. "So to speak, but after a while it became common place and you just thought nothing of it. I kept telling my wife to get

Life as I Lived It

out there on that beach and set those puppies free! Not wanting to be the "odd man out" she did!

Now, if you are in to seeing skin, you could go to the other side of the island where they have total nude beaches. Unfortunately, we didn't have the time to see everything.

Also, at the beginning of the week, there is a social gathering by the pool and club house bar, where free drinks and hordeourves are served. You can socialize and meet your neighbors for the week and make new friends. They also have drawing for prizes and contests to participate in if you're game.

It was here, that I captured the title of "Beer drinking champion of Negril". They were looking for contestants to compete with the current champion and several others. I got up to get another hot dog and the judge started heckling me, trying to get me to join the competition. I shouted back to him, over the crowd that I was of German heritage and that they didn't want me in the contest because I could drink them all under the table and it would be no contest for me.

That really caused some excitement. Now everyone wanted me to prove myself, so into the contest is strode, hotdog in hand. You know those little red hot dogs are very salty. Get my drift?

The champ and all of the contenders lined up across the stage. A twelve oz bottle of Jamaican red stripe beer was placed on the ground at each one's feet. At the command of "GO" all contestants were to pick up their bottle of beer and drink it down. The first to empty his bottle will be the champ.

In the meantime, I ate my hot dog. I was ready! At the word "GO" I picked up my bottle, threw my head back and with wide open mouth poured that bottle in, gushing it down without spelling a drop. I announced "Finished!" And the crowd gasped! The other contestants only had half a bottle drank down. The crowd was astonished, even the judge didn't quite know what to say. I realized the rarity of this moment.

I knew I had them all in the palm of my hand and that I had to seize the moment before it was gone. So I looked around as if looking for something and remarked out loud, "What! Are we only going for one?" At that point the crowd gasped again and the other contestants threw their bottles down in disgust.

I not only triumphed but I blew their minds to boot a double whammy. The judge promptly awarded me a fine bottle of Jamaican coconut rum and the title and status of Beer Drinking Champion of Negril.

I hate to think of how many times people I didn't even know would point me out to others and announce my accomplishment as champs. I had become a celebrity because of it. It seemed everyone knew who I was.

I took the wife out to dinner one evening and the bill was around $1200 Jamaican money. It told her she could never say that I don't spend any money on her!

Life as I Lived It

As far as coins go, in Jamaica, they have only two coins, a ten dollar coin and a twenty dollar coin. The only thing a ten dollar coin would buy was a coke and the twenty dollar coin could buy a beer, otherwise, the coins were useless.

We took a tour with the condo complex activities director as our guide. It was a real interesting tour by van around parts of the area and in the mountains. You got to see how people actually live, everyday life at its best. It made you realize that no matter how bad you think you have it, you are still way above people elsewhere in this world.

As we drove along we would encounter groups of people doing their laundry in small streams near the road or gathered by a faucet in the pipeline that ran alongside of the road. This pipeline was the main water supply to all parts of Jamaica. It simply lay beside the road on top of the ground. Why bury it in a land that has no freezing temperatures? Besides, most islands are volcanic rock only inches beneath the soil, so digging is virtually impossible in most places.

Where ever there were a number of people living, there would be a faucet installed on the pipe for the people to access it. NO homes had running water or indoor plumbing, so you would see people doing their laundry right there at the faucet as well, or filling big five gallon jugs with water and carrying them back to their homes on top of their heads. It reminded me of something you would have seen back in the Egyptian time period.

A great majority of the homes were about the size of a one car garage. In the mountain areas, they were made of bamboo, stood on end and fastened together. You could see right through the house as you passed by. It was common to see people with machetes in one hand and bamboo poles in the other or on their shoulders, walking down the road to their houses. Most building materials were free. You just had to go out and cut it down and take it home!

I asked the guide, "How do these people make a living?" He told me that they do several things to make money. Some work in the sugar cane fields on some of the huge plantations that we passed at the base of the mountains, but those are seasonal jobs. Some make wicker furniture and sell it. They simply sit it beside the road in front of their little house with a "For Sale" sign on it.

Making wicker furniture is a real art. Next time you see some, look at it closely and see how it is woven in such a way to be strong and useful. It takes a lot of time and design to make a quality piece of furniture out of that stuff!

Have you ever wondered what wicker is or where it comes from? I have seen it growing in the mountain jungles. It is a long, uniform in diameter vine that grows from the tree tops and hangs down to the ground. You have to climb the tree, 40 to 50 feet high and cut the wicker vine off, just like a piece of rope and gather it up. It is no easy job.

Some make a living by growing marijuana. Sure, it is illegal, but if you limit yourself to no more than 50 plants the Government considers you to small of a grower to fool with. So, what everyone who grows it does this, they burn a patch of jungle off the side of the mountain and grow 50

Life as I Lived It

plants. The soil is the richest there and it is a pain in the butt to reach, so ono one bothers to destroy it.

Down from the mountains in the low lands, people work regular jobs in the cities when they can find work. The unemployment rate is around 40 percent. Jobs are hard to come by.

I asked our guide, "What is the minimum wage here and how many hours a week do the people commonly work?" He told me that they work a 48 hour work week for which they are paid 50 American equivalent dollars. That is only $1.04 per hour!

We stopped at a Kentucky Fried Chicken for lunch. Chicken is the main meat in Jamaica as well as in a lot of other island countries.

They are terrified of eating beef. It seems that they had an epidemic of mad cow disease many years prior and it left a "bad taste in their mouths", so to speak. As a result, you cannot buy a good steak anywhere and the cattle roam freely where ever they please, no fences anywhere, and they die of old age unless they are hit by a car or truck on the road. Whenever there is a slowdown of traffic, there is usually a cow walking casually down the road, blocking everything up. You get used to it. It is a way of life.

I had noticed that there are very few graveyards. I asked the guide why this was and if they cremated most of the deceased. He told me that when someone dies, they just bury them alongside of the house. No embalming or nothing, not even a marker!

Richard W. Block

I did very much enjoy the beauty of the mountains. The types of plants and trees and flowers were many as well as their colors.

The many varieties of birds were fascinating as well.

Back at the condo one day, I was sitting on the beach watching the activities when Tom came by for a chat. Tom was from Fort Wayne, Indiana.

Every time you talk with someone you usually find out where they are from. We had met and talked previously at the beginning of the week. I had told Tom that I was from the Cincinnati Area, as I often tell people because most people generally know where Cincinnati is as opposed to the Aurora – Lawrenceburg area where I grew up and lived most of my life.

Tom bid me good morning and remarked that I had said that I was from the Cincinnati area. It told him that he was correct in his statement. Then he took me totally by surprise when he next asked if I knew any people in the Lawrenceburg, Indiana area?

I chuckled a little because I knew I had not mentioned I was from that area. I told him, "Well yes, I know just about everybody from that area." Then he asked me if I knew Bobby B.?

(Who had happened to be our state Senator at that time). I said, "Well yes, I know Bobby very well". We worked together at Seagram distilleries for about six years and he was always a nut about baseball and he played on different

Life as I Lived It

softball teams every summer. He is the most avid sports player I have ever known.

Then Tom told me that he and Bobby were roommates at school in Indianapolis for a few years and were "on the outs" with each other for some dumb reason and had not spoken for years. He said he was going to call Bobby on the phone and tell him he had met me and that I was bad-mouthing Bobby. "That might just get them talking again" he said. I told tom to go ahead and be sure to mention my name, because Bobby would know better. Small world isn't it?

Of course, the beach was a world of its own. Many night clubs and bars bordered the beach as well as all kinds of shops. Jamaica has an abundance of craftsmen. They carve all kinds of figures from wood and sell them on the beach. Most of the carvings are done with machetes, knives and chisels. No modern tools because they cannot afford them.

We bought a hand carved sea turtle. There were many colors on the shell. I asked the man who carved it, how he put the colors on it. It was obvious he could not afford or would buy paints or stains to color his carvings. He told me this almost exactly as I had thought. Then he told me he got his coloring from plants and berries that grew locally. "You make do with what you got", was his remark. He was good at his craft. I have that turtle on display in our living room at home and I look at it quite frequently. It reminds me of what people can make, from nothing but things at hand, when they have to, just to make a living.

Richard W. Block

The animal figure designs are also found in hash pipes used for smoking marijuana.

The national wood or tree of Jamaica is the lignum vite. It is a beautiful black and white wood that is very burn resistant. That is why it makes good pipes for smoking. It reminds me of a zebra when both colors are in the same carving.

You see a lot of pipes in the form of porpoises and whales or idols of different face forms. I bought one of the idol figures and I told the man who carved it, that he would do more business if he carved chess pieces instead. He could sell those in sets and make more money.

His carving talent was masterful to say the least. As you walked up and down the beach, "admiring the scenery" if you get my drift, people would hand you menus and program fliers advertising the particular night club or bar you would be passing at this particular time. There was always something happening on the beach.

Every morning when I walked out to the beach, I would be approached by someone selling

Marijuana before I even reach the water's edge. You got used to it; it was a way of life.

I hate to think how many times local people asked me to sell them my binoculars and or my marine radios. Those are the two items that are impossible to come by in Jamaica. They would say "You can get another one when you get home, we cannot get them at all here".

Life as I Lived It

Packs of Marlboro cigarettes are better than money. You cannot get those there either. So if you smoke, take plenty with you. I think two cartons is the limit.

When it comes to adventure though, there is no limit! I would go again!

JOURNEY TO THE PAST

One afternoon my wife and I were driving home from town. We turned onto a parallel side road off the main highway. As we drove along I pointed out each farm and named each farmer who lived there when I was a kid and used to roam the woods and hills in quest of game.

My wife chuckled and said, "Those days are long gone and you will never be able to do those things again as a kid."

I gave her a shocked look and said without hesitation, "you're wrong I can go back forty years in time in the blink of an eye!"

With that said, I closed my eyes and told her this "I can smell the fields of corn and fresh cut hay. I can smell and hear the cattle in the barnyards. I can hear the chickens clucking and the pigs rooting around, as well as smell them. I can hear the birds singing and taste the honeysuckle in the air. I can feel the same grass beneath my feet and the same muddy creek bank that's always been there. I can feel the breeze on my face and hear the same familiar splash of the frogs in the creek. I can almost hear my dog barking after a rabbit. Well, almost, said I.

Life as I Lived It

Do you want to take a time trip? Just close your eyes and let your other senses take you there. Just take care not to be hit by a tractor or kicked by a mule. There's still an entire world out there to be re-enjoyed no matter where your mind's eye takes you. Just close your eyes and see!!!!

JUST FOR LAUGHS

I have always stated that my favorite tool is a hammer in any project.

If you cannot fix it right, you can fix it for good! And if you can't fix it with that hammer, you have got the wrong hammer!!

A lot of the people I work with have cats for pets. They like to talk about them a lot and tell cute stories. After just so much, I like to add to the conversation also, so I declare that I love cats too and I thank they taste just like chicken.

I try to find a little humor in every situation, even the bad ones. Life's too short to be unhappy.

If you really want to see someone else's point of view, put yourself in their shoes and then walk a mile in them. Wait until the next day to determine the results. You may be surprised.

Think about this if you took an object, a book for instance, and laid it in the middle of an empty room, on the floor and then circled it with people of all types and sizes, as you

Life as I Lived It

go around the circle of people you will see that each person has a different view of the same object.

Now you have just learned how to compare points of view on the same object!

KINDERGARTEN

When I was a youngster, my parents would sit at the breakfast table and read the morning newspaper and this fascinated me. What were they doing, looking at these big papers every morning? They were reading. I didn't fully understand, but I wanted to learn how to do what they were doing too. I wanted to learn how to read and write. I was only about four years old at the time. My Mom bought a set of books called Grimm's Fairy Tales. These are what I learned to read and write with. By the time I was five, I could read and write very well. My Mom worked with me every day and I learned fast because I was so fascinated by the process.

When I reached kindergarten age, my mom enrolled me in kindergarten at Southside School.

Aurora had three local public schools, Northside, Westside and Southside. Southside was the only one that offered kindergarten classes.

Southside School was within walking distance from my home, so I walked to school every day. Needless to say, there wasn't a lot my teacher, Mrs. Hotmeyer could teach me that I didn't already know, so I was bored to death most of the time.

Life as I Lived It

She grew to hate me I think, because I was very disruptive in the classroom. I think I held the record for punishments, because I was punished every day without fail!

I was stood in the corners, got my hands slapped with a ruler, paddled on the rump or sent to the principal's office for him to spank me.

One day the teacher put me out of the room, in the hall to stand in the corner, because I still was a disruption in the corner in the classroom!

Well, after a while in the hall corner, I just decided that I was forgotten, so I left and went home. No sooner had I got there, the phone rang and it was the school, looking for me.

The person on the phone said to send me back. The principal was waiting with his paddle as usual. He got used to seeing me so much that we eventually became great friends! It was a friendship that lasted me though the sixth grade, which was the highest grade the school offered before going across town to Junior High School.

We used to bring our sleds to school when there was snow. We had a tall hillside behind Southside School and we would ride down the hill on to the basketball courts, missing the goal posts of course. You surely didn't want to hit one of those goal posts.

I lived close to the school, so I was usually the last one in and the first one out about every day.

Richard W. Block

I was in the third grade one winter and upon arriving at school, there was no one playing outside as usual and I thought it strange. I knew I wasn't late. There was a boy lying on the ice, curled up by the basketball goal post, not moving like he was asleep. I stopped and gazed at him for a moment as I heard my teacher call my name to come on in. I yelled back to her that there was someone lying here on the playground. She said to never mind and come on in to class.

I later found out that the boy had hit the goal post while sledding down the hill and was killed instantly. I did not know him. After that, there were no sleds allowed at school. To this day, I feel sad about it. There was nothing that could have been done to help him.

No parent should outlive their child.

At Easter time we had the "Easter egg roll". Each student brought a colored hardboiled egg to school and one class at a time, the kids would get in a line across the top of the hill behind the school and try to roll their eggs down the hill without breaking them. The first to reach the bottom with an unbroken egg won a prize. I can still see all of us kids, rolling all the eggs, in one mad frenzy down that hill, in my mind, every Easter.

We used to play marbles too. Whatever happened to all those games?

I guess today's technology took over their playtime. That can't be as much fun; it's just a new trend!

LACE-O-FLAGE

Did you ever want to be different? I mean different from everyone else or have things no one else has. Sometimes it's very hard to do. That's why you have to go for, or do things that are in the category of "unique".

I was lucky. I was very artistic, a trait or talent that I inherited from my mother who was very artistic. I also got my photographic memory, sense of humor and my great imagination from her as well.

I remember one time when I had been visiting mom at her home where some construction and excavation had been going on. It had rained previous and everything was total mud in the yard. I was in my car, about to leave, when, as Mom turned to go into the house, she slipped and fell flat on her back in a huge water filled mud hole. I just sat there in my car, looking in disbelief at my mom lying there in that big mud hole. I rolled down my window and shouted to her, "Are you alright"?

She replied, "Aren't you going to help your poor old mother up?"

That was the key phrase – "Poor old Mother".

I instantly knew it was a trap!

I replied, "No way"!

Again she called out, "Aren't you going to help your poor old mother up?"

Again I answered, "No way"! I know you, and I know how you think and I know if I come over there to help you out, you'll pull me in there with you, just so I can return home looking like a big mud ball!"

I'll just stay where I am, thank you very much.

So I just sat there looking at her and she lay there looking at me, then we began laughing. We laughed so hard, we cried. Finally, after we could laugh no more, she got up and went inside and I headed on for home.

That's my mom, that's the way she was. Now, to get back on track, I loved motorcycles and every "bike" I ever owned, I would tear apart and have pieces chromed, put on custom exhausts and accessories, custom gas tanks, chop the fenders, etc. and of course, paint it a color no one else had. But as luck would have it, it wouldn't be long afterwards that the color I so carefully chose would be showing up everywhere! On cars and on other motorcycles as well and it would make me so mad, that I would paint my bike another color. Well, guess what! After a period of time, I'd be in a crowd of vehicles painted that same color too! I

Life as I Lived It

was furious! Why is it that every time I paint my bike some uncommon color, everyone and their brother had to have it too! I was furious!

I thought to myself, "I'm going to have to come up with a paint job that no one can duplicate. I mean no one!! That's when I came up with what I call Lace-o-flage. It was a camouflage pattern using wedding gown lace and two different shades of green, a brown and a black lacquer paint, shot over the lace and then clear coated and buffed out to where it had the appearance of a lake surface that you could almost dive into. It was beautiful as well as unique. I painted my fenders, side covers, fuel tank and two helmets to match.

Everyone who saw my motorcycle was awed by its appearance. People would ask, "Who painted your bike?" I'd reply, "I did it."

Then they would ask. "How much would you take to paint mine like that?" I'd look them in the eye and tell them that there was no amount of money that could get me to paint their bike just like mine. Mine is a one of a kind. No one will ever have on like it. Oh sure, another talented painter might be able to come close, trying to duplicate it, but he would have to have my bike to go by as a pattern, which will never happen! You see, when I sell my bike someday, the paint job doesn't go with it. I will paint it black before I sell it to get a different one. No one but me will ever own this paint job.

Richard W. Block

And that's the way it went. All that exists now is my two helmets with that marvelous paint job on them. People still marvel at them.

With new paints and the disappearance of lacquers, even I could not paint another like it!!

LEARNING HANDGUNS

My ancestors have always been hunters and fishermen.

It has always played a large roll in everyday life especially during the depression in the 11920's and 1930's when jobs and money were hard to come by, so you made do with what you caught or shot.

Needless to say, my relatives were all excellent marksmen with rifles and shotguns.

As times go better, the target turned from live birds to clay bird and paper targets.

Friends and neighbors that my grandfather had taught to hunt and shoot became relatives eventually as families merged through marriages as it often happens in small rural towns.

My Uncles and Cousins were all well-known rifle and shotgun shooters.

My first cousin on my Mother's side, who is a girl, two years younger than I, was a Women's National Trap shooting champion for many years. She used a ten gauge double barrel muzzle loading shotgun. She tried to get into the Men's competition, but she was barred from it because the men were afraid of her.

She could break all 25 birds consistently in a match, which is something few of the men shooters could rarely do. But that's okay because her Dad, my Uncle, took the honors in those matches anyway.

My other Uncles and Cousins were champion shooters as well. Every time I went to one of their homes, I would look at all those silver and gold trophies, plates, cups, plaques and belt buckles on display taking up entire rooms at times.

I would think what a waste of an entire room, with all this "junk" on tables, shelves, walls and floors! It seemed like a huge way of bragging, but what else would you do with all that stuff? Not my cup of tea, not in my home, I thought.

I've always felt that everyone expected me to follow in their footsteps. Those are some tuff footsteps to compete with.

None of my relatives ever thought much of handguns. They thought handguns were pretty much a useless gun unless extremely close on large targets. That's the way to go I thought. No competition from the relatives!

I bought my first handgun when I was fifteen. It was a Walther P-38, 1943 AC code, serial number 2080c which was stolen many years later and has still never been recovered. I still look for it at military gun shows in case it

Life as I Lived It

surfaces. I've probably had a dozen of them since, but that first one has sentimental value.

I soon became a handgun expert. I learned which handguns were accurate and which were not. Some can be improved on and others are just no good at all when it comes to performance.

So I practiced and learned and experimented. With a lot of patience and extreme calmness, I got to be the best pistol shot in my neck of the woods, at least that's the opinion of others who have been witness to some of my strange performances.

I took my boss's friend from work, hunting on a friend's farm with no results one day. We were standing in the barnyard with the farmer drinking a beer that he had given us, when I commented that there was a rabbit in his garden and would he like me to shoot it with my pistol, which I was wearing, for supper?

My boss's friend immediately spoke up and said, "You can't hit that rabbit with a pistol!" My farmer friend said, "No, let him go today." When we finished our beer, I said, "I ought to throw this bottle up and shoot it." Again, my boss's friend said, "you can't throw that bottle up and shoot it with that pistol!" I'll bet you five dollars you can't hit that bottle! No, I'll give you five dollars if you can hit that bottle!"

Standing by the fence I threw the bottle as high in the air as I could and I yelled, "Is that high enough?" When I

Richard W. Block

heard him say yeah, I pulled my pistol and fired one shot shattering the bottle into pieces as it fell.

I turned and saw the shocked look on my boss's friend's face as he reached for his wallet. I said, "You don't have to pay me the five dollars, I just wanted you to learn a lesson." He said, "No, No, you take the five dollars, it was worth it to see the shot." As I took the money from his hand, the farmer said to him "Mister, I would not have bet five dollars on that shot, I'd been surprised if he'd missed it!"

I used to love to throw things up and shoot them. I could hit quarters, but I always had trouble hitting pennies. Quarters got a little expensive so I quit that.

LENTZ

In 2002, my wife Edie, I and my close friend Brett, went to Germany, just to tour around and see the sights. One of the many things on our list that we wanted to see, was the bridge at Remmagen, on the Rhine River. Well, guess what, there is no bridge there anymore. It collapsed in 1945, during World War II and was never rebuilt. The four huge pillars still stand, two on each side of the Rhine River. The bridge was a railroad bridge and it connected Remmagen to Lentz. You can cross by ferry if you want to go to Remmagen, so we took the ferry and crossed over to see the town and tour the museum they built in the towers on the Remmagen side of the Rhine River.

Later, when we returned to the Lentz side, we decided to have lunch in the tavern in the center of Lentz.

Each town has one tavern, which is the "hub of the wheel" in the Zentrum. Zentrum means center in German, where only foot traffic or bicycles are allowed and no cars. Usually there is a fountain and/or trees and benches to sit and enjoy the day on a laid brick road surface.

We three went into the tavern and sat down at a table. I told my wife and friend Brett to not say a word, that I would do all the talking. My German is good enough to express my wishes without giving me away as an American.

The waitress arrived with the menus and asked for our drink order. I asked what was on tap and ordered two beers and a cola. While the waitress was getting the drinks, I was translating the menu to Edie and Brett. When she returned with the drinks, she asked what we would like to have. I told her I didn't see what I wanted on the menu. She asked me what is that I wanted. I told her I wanted wurst, mashed potatoes and sauerkraut. She said she would check with the kitchen and see if it was available and left. When she returned, she said that yes, we have that. Then she looked to my wife Edie for her order and Edie said in English, "I don't see anything I want". At that, the waitress said in a raised voice, "Oh! English!", and then scurried off, only to return with the manager, who spoke a little English. He handed Edie and Brett some different menus printed in English. Edie said with disgust, "I will have what he is having", referring to me. The Manager asked, "Well what is he having?"

And she told him what I had ordered. He then said, "I'm sorry, we don't have that here." "You must order from the English menu!" "Just point to the number, listing your choice and the waitress will get it?" So she and Brett ordered hamburgers and fries.

I told Edie and Brett that it is going to be interesting to see what the waitress brings. Well, a short time later, here comes the waitress with a big tray containing my wurst, mashed potatoes and sauerkraut and their hamburgers and fries.

Edie said, "You're eating my burger and fries and I'm eating your food and at that she switched the plates of food around. I said, "Don't blame me!" "You're the one who opened your big English speaking mouth, when I told you not to speak and that only I was going to do the talking."

I really didn't mind. It was all a learning adventure. I am ready to go again!

LIFE'S LITTLE QUIRKES

Do you frequently encounter someone you grew up with, childhood friend, a classmate, etc. that you have not seen in a few years and are quite shocked at their appearance?

You look at them and wonder, Do I look as old, or as terrible, or as decrepit, or as great (you choose the befitting word according to the individual and great usually never comes to mind), as they look to me?

Then you wonder do they recognize me? Should I approach them and renew old friendships? Unless they give some sign of recognition, you usually just move on and say nothing. That is usually the case.

It can be really baffling when someone approaches you and talks to you, who obviously knows you pretty well and you have no idea who they are, especially when someone with you asks who that was and you say you have no idea what so ever!

Changes to yourself happen day by day and you see them in the mirror every morning while getting ready for your work day to begin, which you take in stride with little

Life as I Lived It

concern. Changes to others, which you have not seen for a while, happen all of a sudden it seems.

When reality really hits home, is when you attend you class reunion. It has been 330-35 years since you graduated and you find yourself among a crowd of strangers. (So they appear).

You make the remark, "Look at all these old people". Your spouse replies, "Well, you are the same age they are". (Providing you have a spouse and they are still with you).

It is strange how people never consider themselves to be old like their classmates and the first words out of their mouth at this point are, "Gee, do I look that old too?" Of course the replies will vary, depending on how kind your spouse wants to be to you in comparison to the others present.

Some people move fare away and you never see them again to you these people will always be as you remember them, forever young.

Just think, that is how they remember you!!

Sometimes, I think I would like to move far away, never to return. That way, I will never see my friends, relatives and neighbors grow old and pass on. The will always be frozen in time in my mind and safe from life's harms.

Isn't life a Bitch?!!!!!

LITTLE ROCK, BIG LESSON

When I was a boy of twelve years, I found myself I the Smokey Mountains with the Boy Scouts at a campground named Smokemont.

A mountain stream ran by it and a waist deep swimming hole was formed by piling rocks to dam up the flowing waters. A number of campers, over a few camping seasons, each adding rocks, had accomplished this.

Our southern Indiana troop came here about every three years. We passed had bills (sale flyers) every week to earn our way. If you didn't pass the hand bills, you didn't get to go on the trips, so I got to know about every house and street in our town of Aurora.

I was down a path to the swimming hole, when I encountered several fellow scouts throwing rocks at a hornets nest with no luck of hitting it. A hornet's nest is a hollow globe shaped hive that looks as if it was made from old newspapers about basketball size.

Life as I Lived It

Without thinking, I joined in the fun and scored at direct hit breaking the nest open and releasing hundreds of very mad hornets.

We ran away quickly without being stung. A hornet has a vicious sting and can sting many times and they were ready to prove it! A few hours later fellow scouts were returning to camp with festering hornet stings looking for first aid relied.

Word had reached my scoutmaster that I was the marksman with the rock and I instantly achieved the top of his black list!

Our scoutmaster, Buck, adorned himself with netting and armed with a can of fuel oil, dowsed the nest remnants and drove away the hornets. Buck was a brave man. He never said much about the incident to me. Sometimes unspoken spankings are worse than a well-deserved chewing out.

MAGIC SKUNK PART I

While returning to my boss's lodge outside of Grayling, Michigan, I happened upon a lone baby skunk, walking along the roadside in the dark. I could see he would probably be another victim of the highway in short order, so I stopped and gave him a lift with the help of a paper bag.

He was unafraid. He'd never encountered man before. Skunks are usually unafraid anyway.

They are a very nearsighted night animal that depends on his nose more than anything.

When you find a lone baby it's usually because its' mother is dead due to rabies or the highway. Just lost, is the least likely. I handled him with gloves until I deemed him safe.

My boss was entertaining guests, one of whom was a well-known magician. A show was requested and I was to help set it up, supplying table, chairs, coins, cards, etc. He said, "I need a small animal. I have doves, but not with me. How about your skunk? Will he bit?"

I said, "No". So, a quick practice went well.

Life as I Lived It

The guests sat shoulder to shoulder around the table as he performed amazing tricks. At one point he would be pulling yards of crepe paper from his mouth with both hands, mounding the paper into a huge pile in front of him and then with only one hand pulling the paper. While using only the one hand, the other hand was behind his back, where I stood, awaiting the skunk to be slipped into his hand. The skunk didn't want to go! After some determined tries, he went, under protest I could tell.

He brought the skunk up between himself and the table, beneath and into the huge pile of crepe paper tumbling the whole mess into a ball while exclaiming magical words and landing it in the center of the table. The pile started moving and out walked the skunk tail held high. Everyone was excited!!!

Seconds later, everyone realized the skunk was more excited than they, clearing the lodge and ending the show! A star is born!!!

MAGIC SKUNK PART II

After the cleanup from the exciting skunk show, the magician headed for the forest to sit alone in his portable deer stand we had erected earlier and watch for animals while the embarrassment and skunk smell faded away.

I took some of the guests to shoot clay pigeons while the lodge aired out.

While returning I could see the lone magician, sitting in his tree off in the distance. I thought to myself, what an opportunity to poke a little fun at this city fellow!!

I sent my gear on ahead to the lodge and slipped silently into the brush, creeping close without notice, hiding in a dense brush pile. It was late and the light was fading fast. I knew he would soon be returning to the lodge. I let out with the growl only a wolverine would make and shook the bushes. Everything went quiet. Even the birds stopped singing. Sound carries well in a pine forest. He looked around frantically. I growled and shook more fiercely. I heard him descend the rope ladder with great speed, hit the ground and run like a rabbit, turning on the gravel road and running for the lodge. I ran parallel with him

Life as I Lived It

concealed by the brush and dim light. As he reached the edge of the lodge he stopped and peered into the forest. I was there lying in the brush, growling and shaking the brush fiercer than before.

I could see his eyes. They were as large as golf balls! And just as white!! As he heaved a large rock, landing a few yards ahead of me, I held my hands over my mouth to keep from laughing. I was growling meaner than ever, when all of a sudden, thud!!! A big rock lands a foot from my nose!! At that, I burst out laughing. He called out, "Block is that you? You scared the hell out of me! Don't you ever tell anyone about this!" It was great!!!

MAUSER 98K

My dad had a bother, Lloyd and three sisters, Mae, Margie and Betty.

My dad's mother died in childbirth while having Betty. Betty was given up for adoption and was never heard from again until after World War II had ended and she was grown and married.

One thing they all had in common was that they all had a hand in the War and that they all returned home to the same house.

This meant that everything they brought back from the war, mostly would up being left in storage at the old family house on Market Street, where I grew up as a child, because it was their father's house at the time.

Since the beginning of time, the Block family and its relatives have fought in the thick of battles in every major war with no losses of life. There were plenty of wounds but no deaths.

My dad was first sergeant in the 83rd Infantry Division, Signal Corp. His brother Lloyd was a bombardier and

Life as I Lived It

gunner in the Army Air Corp. Mae's husband, Delbert, was a Tech Sergeant in the 45th Thunderbird Division. Margie's husband, Bob, was a Petty Officer in the Navy. Betty's husband, Dave, I'm not sure about. Well anyway, among all the German flags, armbands, bayonets, swords, pistols, hand grenades, shell casings, bullets, photographs, etc. was the German Mauser 98K rifle that my Uncle Delbert took from the biggest "Kraut" he ever saw in his life, so he told me.

He said his division was pushing through Germany toward the Eagles Nest when he saw the huge German solider lying in a ditch beside the road, clutching a brand new Mauser rifle, so he jumped out of his halftrack and grabbed it up.

Later on, when the opportunity arose, he sent the rifle home after dunking it in a grease solution to preserve it and there it lay in the attic for all those years until I dug it out. I cleaned the grease off and played with it all the time as I grew.

One day dad grabbed the old rifle and said, "If you're going to play with this, I'm going to cut the firing pin off so it can't shoot. There are too many shells lying around and you might get hurt if you stuck one of them in there and it wasn't the right one, and you got it to go off!

So that's what he did.

As I got to be a teenager, I took the rifle to a gunsmith and had it repaired. Well, repairing the old firing pin was not the way to go, because it misfired occasionally.

Richard W. Block

As I got a little older, about 15 or 16 years old, my resources got a little better and I was able to get a new firing pin and put it in myself. I used to buy war surplus ammo at the rate of five dollars for a hundred rounds. You can't buy it for that price anymore! I got very adept at using those five round stripper clips. It was a really great rifle and I loved shooting it.

I soon found out that it was no fun shooting tin cans. You could sit a can on a fence post and shoot all day at it and never knock it off. The armor piercing rounds would pass right through the can like it wasn't even there, leaving a perfect round hole but not moving the can at all. It sure would blow concrete blocks and big rocks into small pieces though! Those bullets would shoot through trees of most sizes, steel bridge structures and railroad rails, like punching paper!

I used to hunt groundhogs with the rifle, the sights adjusted up to two thousand meters. I used to think that nothing was too far away to shoot at. All I had to do was elevate the sights to the proper distance and I was in business! I'd sneak up to the edge of a field and catch a groundhog sunning himself on his mound, way out there. I'd take careful aim and that would be the end of that. After a while, I found it more fun to blow the mound, out from under the groundhog than to shoot the groundhog himself.

It was hilarious. One minute he'd be sunning himself on his mound, enjoying the day, and the next second, he'd be running around, amidst a cloud of dirt and dust, wondering what the heck caused his mound to explode!

Life as I Lived It

He'd just run around in a state of confusion, looking at everything. I'd be rolling around on the ground, laughing like some madman, on the other side of the field.

Then came the encounter with the gar. I had seen a groundhog disappear into his den and I was sitting on a log at the field's edge, waiting him out. I was just sitting there, taking in the scenery, when I noticed something out in the creek, cutting through the water with lightning speed.

It was a gar zipping up and down the creek like a rocket powered shark, his top fin slicing through the water like a knife. I stood up and flipped the safety off on the Mauser.

It was fun to shoot things in the water with the armor piercing rounds. I had shot in the water many times and when the round hits the water, it creates a suction, where the water actually recesses down for an instant and then whooshes upwards of eight to ten feet high like a geyser! I thought; wait till that gar flies by again. Won't he get a surprise! Well, there he came, zipping along at that lightning speed of his. I crossed over him with the sights of the Mauser leading him nearly a foot and ka-pow! The water blew high in the air, but with no result. Missed, I thought, but I was sure I was on target. Back came the gar again and I passed over him with the sights once more, leading him nearly a foot and ka-pow! Again the water blew high in the air, and again it was a miss! I couldn't believe I missed, I know I was on target.

I bolted another round into the chamber as the gar started his third pass, zipping through the water like lightning.

Again I passed over him with the Mauser's sights, leading him by a foot.

Ka-pow, the water blew high into the air for the third time, clearly, another miss!

I checked my sights as the gar turned around for another pass. One hundred meters was the setting. That's just where they're supposed to be. Nothing wrong there I thought.

It was that moment it hit me. Optical illusion! I was on target all right! I didn't allow for the optical illusion factor of the target being under water! The gar was actually a foot deeper in the water than he appeared, I was shooting over him!

I bolted another round into the chamber as the gar made top speed, cutting through the water like a rocket. I passed under him by a foot this time, with the Mauser's sight leading him by the usual foot. Ka-pow! We have life off! As the water blew high into the air, so did the gar! He went flying through the air like a missile, landing on his back and cutting through the water like a speed boat until he came to a stop. Then he sank to the bottom.

Wow! What a show! That was the biggest gar I ever saw!

I took the first deer I ever killed with that rifle too. It was a record ten point buck. I don't know why, but I guess I just got out of the habit of shooting that rifle as time passed and I got into other things of interest.

Life as I Lived It

I think the last time I shot that rifle was a few years ago at scout camp, when I needed to clear the road of some huge buried rocks that were causing a problem.

You could hardly drive down the road without dragging your vehicle bottom on them, so I blew few chunks out of them with a few armor piercing rounds. They were far too massive to dig up and I felt that this was a simple fix. Besides, I got no arguments from anybody.

MEMORIES OF SUMMER CAMP

I was born and grew up on the edge of a small Indiana town on the Ohio River, where as I grew, I learned all the outdoor skills of hunting, fishing and trapping. The river and creeks was a playground for my cousins and me.

Long about 1956, I reached the age of 8 and joined the Cub Scouts which led to the Boy Scouts at age eleven, a natural thing to do of course, because of the outdoor program and skills the Boy Scouts practice.

My Scoutmaster was a strict and demanding man, when he barked, you jumped. His name was Buck C., a finer man I've never met. I shared many campfires with Buck and a lot of who I am, I owe to him.

Somewhere around 1962, our troop, number 37 was at Camp Louis Ernst, our home for one week each summer every year. As events happen, I was hiking one of the many trails to our campsite when I encountered the "possum". He was about half grown and unafraid and so was I. He ran, I chased. I'd handled many "possums" in my days of hunting and trapping, so I thought nothing of grabbing him by the tail and taking him to camp with me. After

Life as I Lived It

a day or two of being handled by dozens of scouts, "Mr. Possum" became quite harmless and friendly. Riding around on everyone's shoulders was common place.

Family night was Friday and the huge camp lodge was filled with scouts and parents. In I walked with "possum" on my shoulder. Everyone wanted to hold him and so he passed from shoulder to shoulder.

While perched on one scout's shoulder he "let go" right down the back of his uniform shirt just like squirting mustard bottle and just as yellow! All of a sudden he was standing alone in the middle of the floor, yelling. "Get him off! Get him off!!" Everyone was laughing as he gave me the "possum" and I put him on my shoulder.

Buck came over to me and said, "I thought you had that "possum" trained!" Then I said, "I do!" as I turned my back and pointed while exclaiming "you don't see anything on my back!!"

He was speechless and turned and walked away. That was the only time I ever saw him do that. Normally he would have a return comment. I think he was laughing under his breath, but didn't want anyone to know it.

MICHIGAN DEER SEASON

From the late 1970's through the 80's I used to love to go to Grayling, Michigan for the opening days of rifle season for deer.

Why there, instead of the rich farm lands and better hunting of home?

Well, it wasn't to just go and hunt deer; it was for the excitement and environment.

Michigan's rifle season always opens on November 15th each year, regardless of what day of the week it falls on.

Indiana, like some of the other states, move the opening day date to fall on a Saturday each year.

What's the difference, you're probably wondering? The difference is the number of hunters in the field. Hell, everybody and their brother are out hunting on opening day if it falls on a non-work day like Saturday, right?

Most of the population of Michigan lives in the lower part of the state and they would usually have to take a week's

Life as I Lived It

vacation from work to hunt. If the season opened in the middle of the week or so, most people don't want to waste the first three or four days of their vacation sitting around in a cabin waiting for the season to open, so they wait until the week end to go hunting, even though the season has already opened.

That means fewer hunters in the field on opening days of certain years.

I've always estimated one hunter for each acre in the state! That's a lot of people out there hunting, all at one time.

As you travel North from the big cities in the lower parts of the state the C.B. Radio would be "humming" from all the hunters traveling to their favorite hunting areas, all talking about past hunts and telling stories.

Some of those stories could be classified as "tall tales", to say the least, but they were always entertaining and made the travel time pass quickly.

It was interesting to see all sorts of vehicles, cars, trucks, campers, some pulling trailers with A.T.V's or snowmobiles or camping gear, but all displaying hunter orange garments in the windows and on the people inside the vehicles.

It was like an invading army! And on opening day you knew it was an invading army!!

You would be sitting out in the woods opening day in the dark of the morning and just as soon as it almost got light enough to see, the shooting would start.

You were allowed to use any caliber rifle, .22 center fire and up, with a five round magazine maximum. If you had a shell in the chamber that made six shots you would have in your rifle.

It was like a war movie, when the troops were hitting the beach! It would seem like every hunter who fired, fired every round in his rifle as if the deer was running and he missed every time, because some other hunter would do the same, and then another and another. You could actually tell which way a deer was going! What lousy shooters those guys are, I'd think to myself!

You were not allowed by law to use tree stands so you hunted on the ground from a blind. The usual tactic was to dig a fox hole at the base of a big tree and sit on the rim of the hole with your back against the tree and your feet in the hole. If the bullets got to close for comfort, you just simply dropped down into the fox hole for protection. When I'd think of it, I'd count the shots. Sometimes I'd count over two hundred shots between daylight and ten a.m.!

Between hunting hours and in the evening, the towns and markets would be packed with orange clad people shopping.

Most small towns had a "buck pole". All the shops would donate prizes and the hunters would hang their deer on the buck pole for display. The contest would only run for the first and second days of the season.

There were prizes for the first deer brought in; the deer killed by the youngest hunter, the first deer brought in by

Life as I Lived It

a woman, etc. and of course the largest scoring antlers, using the Boone and Crocket scoring system. This prize was usually a new rife and scope. Some buck contests had several dozen categories! That's a lot of prizes.

I always ran into town around noon to see what was on the Buck pole. It was always an interesting experience.

I'd go into town and hang out in the bars in the evening. I would sit next to a table full of hunters, chugging down their beers and telling of the day's hunt to each other. On guy would say he saw a couple of deer, but got no shots. Another would say he saw only does and no bucks. Others saw none.

One guy said he got off a couple of sound shots but didn't hit anything. What a dangerous idiot that guy is, I thought to myself!

A sound shot is when a person hears something in the bushes, but can't see anything, so he shoots at the noise area anyway. I wonder how shocked he'd be if he hit what was making the noise and discovered he'd just killed one of his buddies!

I'd like to know where those guys are hunting so I can be sure to avoid that area.

Then I'd go back to the cabin and turn on the eleven o'clock news and listen to the casualty reports. They would report the deaths and then the wounded.

It's amazing how 90% of the injuries are self-inflicted! He was putting his gun in the car and it went off, or in the trunk and it fires, or was getting it out of the car or trunk or gun rack and so on and it just went off!! Some of them slipped and fell or dropped their gun and it went off. Others were crossing fences when it happened or were handing it to someone or it was being handled to them.

I remember one man shot and killed his son while getting his rife from the back seat of his car, where his son was sitting as well. That's a good example of poor gun handling guidelines and procedures.

I remember another instance where a man was killed at ten o'clock in the evening, while sitting at a table in cabin playing cards with his hunting buddies, when a bullet came through the window hitting him in the head.

That always struck me as more of an assassination than an accident.

Then you have your heart attack hunters who were simply out of shape physically.

Wow. How tragic, but this is pretty common every season. Things would calm down though after the first couple of days of hunting to a common routine.

Why then you're probably wondering? Well, it's because people, especially hunters, are a creature of habit. They come to the woods early in the morning, leave for lunch around ten a.m. or so, return around 2 p.m. or so, and leave for the evening at dark.

Life as I Lived It

Deer are not stupid. They are very smart. After the first couple of days of hunting, they have the hunters schedule all figured out, so they adjust their feeding and moving around schedules to avoid confronting the hunters. As a result: The hunters see less deer and shoot less as well. The deer purposely see to it themselves!

There was some public hunting land near our cabin. I would slip up to the bordering dirt road where all the hunters parked their vehicles and find a spot to sit down and watch where I wouldn't be noticed.

The hunters would park along the road around daylight and go through their morning ritual of door slamming, coughing, talking, crushing out cigarettes, tying their boot laces, throwing cans and bottles around, jacking shells into their guns and tramping off into the woods to where they were going to hunt.

I'd just sit perfectly still and wait. After everything settled down and all was quiet the deer would come filtering out of the woods and stand there by the cars and trucks, looking back into the woods, in the direction of where the hunters had gone only moments before!

I'm talking about anywhere from 6 to 10 deer at a time! If I saw one I wanted, I'd just drop him where he stood and the rest would run off to protected areas and hide out the rest of the day.

Of course, the hunters would hear my shot which was near where their vehicles were parked and come running to see what had happened. So, I'd tell them how I got a deer, courtesy of themselves and their habits.

Well the next day I'd change my tactics. I knew that after I told them how I got a deer, they would all be sitting along the road at the woods edge, waiting for the deer to come out, which is exactly what they did!

You'd think they would figure out after a while, that if some of them don't enter the woods as usual, the deer won't be coming out! It didn't take the deer any time at all to figure out that the hunters were not coming in, but staying on the edge. So, the deer would just slip away, deeper into the woods where "you know who" was waiting. I'd pick one out and drop him.

The hunters would hear the shot and come to see what happened. I'd tell them how they provided me with more deer again and thank them for their help.

As I left, I informed them that the woods would be all theirs for the rest of the season, because I had all the meat I needed and I was putting my gun away. I left them all standing mumbling to each other.

Sometimes you just have to play the part when the stage is set, I thought to myself.

As time goes on, things change and I didn't hunt in Michigan anymore for about 15 plus years, but I missed it. So, 3 or 4 years ago I came back and hunted again.

Life as I Lived It

Things had really changed. There were few Buck Poles to be found. There was nowhere near the volume of hunters and I counted less than 30 shots on opening day.

I guess when the old timers passed on; they took the fun and excitement with them.

MICROWAVE EXPERIMENTS

I worked for Mcdonalds' Restaurants for twenty five years. I hired in as a second assistant manager in late 1971 and learned the business from the ground up.

Mcdonalds had a hand shake contract with a meat processing company in North Baltimore, Ohio that supplied all the frozen meat patties for several states of McDonald Restaurants exclusively.

I toured their meat plant several times and they are very protective of their processing equipment and processes. They have top secret stuff that they developed themselves in house.

The plant is located there simply because there is a Nitrogen Plant next door and they have a direct pipeline from the Nitrogen Plant into their meat processing facility. The nitrogen is used to flash freeze each individual meat patty. You have to see it to believe it.

We would receive regular deliveries of meat patties in 30 pound case by way of a refrigerated semi-trailer truck.

Life as I Lived It

At that time, McDonald's sandwich production involved a holding bin that was heated to keep the complete sandwiches warm and fresh for vending. The sandwiches were timed with time cards and were not kept there over ten minutes. If a sandwich was ten minutes old and not sold, it was put in a completed waster container and counted up at the end of the day before being thrown out to the trash.

I used to take a variety of these waste sandwiches home and experiment with them using a microwave oven.

I wanted to see if I could bring a sandwich that had been refrigerated or frozen for a length of time, back to its' original hot and fresh condition.

I found that any sandwich that contained dill pickle slices on it, had to have the pickles removed or the microwaved pickles would sour the whole sandwich

Also, some of the mac and tartar sauces didn't taste exactly the same, so they were better scraped clean as well. Other than those two problems, things heated well as could be expected.

My goal was to present a program to the Corporation where McDonalds Restaurants could put all their completed sandwiches that didn't sell, into the freezer in special containers and freeze them. When the refrigerated meat trucks made their delivery, they could pick up the frozen product and take it to where it could be kept frozen and shipped overseas to some of the countries that were starving and needed the food.

Unfortunately the powers that be declared there were too many legal ramifications.

What if someone was to get sick on the food? There would be all kinds of legal problems.

I felt it was a workable plan and still do.

It all boils down to the old adage that, "Behind every successful man, stands someone telling him he's wrong every step of the way".

MIRACLES

As I am sitting here in the Florida Keys at a friend's home, it has all of a sudden started raining. The usual breeze has stopped and the water is just pouring from the valley in the roof, splashing down onto a big flat stepping stone in the flower bed, where it splatters everywhere and soaks into the ground.

It reminds me of a movie called "Blast from the Past", where a young man in his 30's was born and lived in a fall-out shelter and had never experienced the outside world. I can still picture him sitting on a park bench in the rain and one of his new found friends with an umbrella, came up to him and asked him if he had ever heard the expression, "too dumb to come in out of the rain"?

His reply was that his father was a scientist and he said that everything is a miracle and until now, he really couldn't understand what his father meant.

Everything is a miracle.

I know there are scientific reasons behind everything that happens, but that doesn't make things any less of a miracle.

Richard W. Block

The rain has stopped. The breeze is picking up again and the sun is starting to peak through the white and grey bunches of clouds floating by.

We take so many things for granted that we don't take time to stop and "smell the roses", as to say.

I was taking one of the company executives, (who thought he was a hunter) hunting one day. As we were walking along in the woods, he all of a sudden stopped and remarked, "Look at that tree! Isn't it beautiful? I bet it is really old. It was probably here before the Indians were and saw them pass by the same as us."

You know.... I had really never thought of it in that way. Maybe he was more of an outdoorsman than I had given him credit for. That hunt and that statement forever changed my life in the way that I looked at things. "I couldn't see the forest because of the trees". Well now I could. There was a beauty always there, that I never took the time to notice or really appreciate and I have been in those woods all my life!

I guess you could compare that to sleeping through the best part of a movie.

As I look up from my writing, I see the sky is again blue with new clean white cloud formations floating by. The distant sound of thunder has faded far away and the birds are beginning to sing. I wonder if they are singing about the glorious day that is beginning to unfold before their eyes. It is a miracle.

Life as I Lived It

It is spring and the flowers and shrubbery are blooming. Things in the world of plant life are awakening and coming to life. The grass is getting greener and the leaves are sprouting everywhere.

The farther north you go, the more the snow is melting.

Snow... now there is another one of nature's miracles. Those snow white flakes, floating down and turning everything to clean and white. It can be so beautiful in some respects and a pain in the butt in another respect, because you have to go out and shovel it off your walk

Brrrr….. it's cold out there!

The next thing you know, it is spring. The snow is gone and everything is green and growing.

Then it is summer and hot in the sun. Oh, to just find a shady cool place with a breeze to sit and enjoy the day.

The next thing you know, your shoveling that snow again, providing you are not in the sunny south!

The change of the seasons, another of nature's miracles, is something that has occurred since the beginning of time. I suppose it is a miracle that I am here to witness it all and perhaps appreciate some of it.

MONKEY SEE, MONKEY DO!

When my son, Mike, became of driving age, I bought him a pick-up truck. He was always driving mine and I figured, the only way I'm going to be able to use my own truck is to get him one of hi s own, so I bought him a little dodge ram 50 pick-up truck. It differed a little from my full size Chevy, by being smaller and being a standard shift, as opposed to my automatic.

I had taught him to ride motorcycles, so a standard shift was old hat to him.

He was soon out of school and had a job making pretty fair wages, so it wasn't long before he bought himself other trucks that he liked better.

He seemed to favor the Toyota 4 wheel drive pick-ups, because he had two of them that he switched back and forth driving.

One day I needed a ride from somewhere, back to my car, which was parked at my place of employment.

It was a ride I will never forget.

Life as I Lived It

When we came to a stoplight, he would push the clutch pedal down and put the stick shift in neutral and let the clutch pedal up, then kept revving the motor until the light changed green, at which time he would push the clutch pedal down, shift to first gear and then proceed on.

As he shifted to higher gears he would let off the gas to idle while shifting and when he let the clutch petal up, it would throw you forward in your seat, at which time he would push the gas, throwing you backwards in your seat.

This happened with every shift of the gears, I wondered who he learned this from.

I knew where he learned the procedure of putting the vehicle in neutral while at a stoplight. He got that from watching me, which brings to mind this story.

The newlyweds were settled in at their new home. The wife decided she would bake a ham for her husband for their evening meal. When the ham was brought to the table for him to carve, it didn't look like the same piece of meat they had bought at the supermarket only the day before. The wife had trimmed the end off, making it much smaller. He asked, "why did you trim the ham in such a manner?" Her reply was, "that's the way my mother always did it."

A short time later they were at a family gathering and the man asked his mother-in-law about the ham baking procedure and her reply was, "that's the way my mother did it." So, they went to his wife's grandmother and asked her the same question and her reply was, "well, I had to trim the ham in that manner because that was the size of my baking pan!"

Now that I have told you that story, you will be able to relate to the rest of this one.

When we reached my parked car, I told mike to hop out and take a ride with me.

We climbed into my little Chevy Nova and I said to him, "Mike, I've been watching you drive and I can see that you are using my bad habits, in the way that you drive. Today, I'm going to set you straight."

I started my car and proceeded on as I spoke, "you see, this little car of mine has some problems which I compensate for. The first is, it has a fluid operated clutch system, which has a small leak. It only leaks when there is pressure in the system, such as when I have the clutch pedal pushed down, while sitting at a red light. I never could find the leak, so I just put it in neutral and let the clutch pedal up, so I don't use so much fluid. I just fill the reservoir less often this way. Secondly, the motor likes to die, so I keep it revved up. So it is ok to keep the clutch pedal pushed down and leave it in gear when you are at a stop light in your truck."

I don't know where you got your shifting from, but here is how you shift, and I proceeded to shift gears showing him how shift smoothly just like an automatic transmission does it.

The next time I rode with Mike, I noticed his driving skills had improved immensely.

It was just like, well, riding with myself.

MOVIES AND CONCERTS

I like going to the movies and concerts as many people do as well. The difference between me and others is that I get a lot more from an event than the majority of the others do.

How can that be you asked? Well, let me tell you a story that will change your outlook on movies and concerts.

McDonald's owner Mr. "G" used to purchase season tickets at a local concert theater. There were a total of 4 seats available at most every performance for the employees to request and use at no cost, if they wanted to go see a particular group perform.

The secretary who divided up the tickets and frequently attended concerts herself, asked me one day, how the concert was that I had attended the night before. I told her it was really great!!

She had seen this group perform before and commented that they might give a good performance, but not a really great one.

I said, "Do you take your binoculars with you when you go to concerts?" She replied, "No you are sitting in seats only a few rows from the center of the stage". "What do I need binoculars for?"

I said, "To watch the show I take a pair of 10x50 binoculars with me to every performance I attend"! She laughed and remarked, "That's the stupidest thing I ever heard. What good are they so close to the stage? What do you need them for?"

Again I said, "To watch the show! I'm talking about the other show. The one you don't even know is going on unless you have a good pair of binoculars!"

Then I questioned her about previous concerts she had attended. Did you see all those autographs on Willie Nelson's guitar?" She said, "Well I couldn't make out the names but I could see something all over his guitar". I said, "Well I could see every name", and named them for her, as well as the name of the manufacturer of his guitar, which was on a label inside of it!"

"Did you watch the men in black running around in the rafters, adjusting and operating the spotlights?" Did you see the stagehand slip the drummer that glass of water from behind the stag? Did you see the musician's girlfriends, wives and family members on the end of the stage in the dark, watching the show? Did you see the stagehands scurrying around, dressed in black, setting up props for the next song set?

Did you read the logo on the Ted Nugent's hat or what was printed on some of the bands shirts? Did you see

Life as I Lived It

the look in that girls eyes from the audience when she gave the flower to the lead singer and he leaned down and kissed her?

Of course you didn't! You just sit there like a person with tunnel vision watching only the main show and have no idea of what is really going on. What's the point in going to a concert if you are only going to watch part of it?

"Well!" She said. "I don't care to see that thing!" "That's fine," I said, "you go watch a good concert and I'll go see the same one, but for me it will be a really great one!"

I think she took binoculars with her after that.

The difference between the cinemas and the concerts is that you only have the audience's reactions, as a second performance to watch, in addition to the actual movie being shown on the big screen.

It's amazing and sometimes hilarious, how people react to different scenes on the big screen. There is a whole performance to see and listen to there. It's interesting how different generations react differently to the same scene.

Most people only watch the movie. They're afflicted with tunnel vision and will never know what they are missing.

MUSIC AND YOUTH

As a lad of nine in the 4th grade, I took up playing the drums in the Southside School Band.

I dropped out of band though, as I entered the fifth grade. I discovered it had become an after school activity instead of getting you out of other classes during school hours.

I lived about a block away from school. I was usually the last one to get to school and the first to leave. When that bell rang, I was gone! Roaming the hills with gun and dog seeking adventure, that's for me.

As time passed, I learned to regret dropping out of band.

As a Boy Scout, I would marvel at my friends who were band members and could play the bugle. About four of them would take turns blowing bugle calls at different ceremonies, they could rally play well.

As more time passed, we grew into manhood and went our own ways seeking "fame and fortune".

Life as I Lived It

I stayed with the boy scouts, becoming a leader and serving on committees.

Something else stayed as well, the bugle, and with no one to play it. It was donated to the troop by one of the previous buglers' father. It was a beauty. It was chromed with a trumpet mouthpiece. I guess the previous bugler felt more at home using the same type of mouthpiece as on his trumpet in band.

I would toot around on it from time to time and discovered I could probably learn how to play it if I really set my mind to it.

I bought a bugle from a friend of mine in the army surplus business and kept it in my car. I had an hour drive to work and an hour drive home that is two hours of practice each day if I stuck with it.

I soon found myself at a music store, buying a trumpet mouthpiece for it. The mouthpiece cost as much as the bugle! It made all the difference in the world though. Later I found that a coronet mouthpiece fit better.

After a year or so and a lot of practice, miles later, I found myself playing the bugle at events and ceremonies and teaching others to play as well.

I still do not read music. I play by ear as do a lot of people. An U.S. Army bugle call tape became my music book. I learned so much about the bugle that I made my own tape.

MUZZLE BLAST

Bob B. and I were at the Boy Scout Camp Rifle Range one afternoon and we were going to show the scouts how to shoot muzzle loading rifles. I wasn't paying that much attention to Bob until I saw him pulling the ramrod out of his rifle after ramming a load down the barrel of his rifle. I happened to think, and the asked him if he still had a load in the barrel from last year's deer season? He thought for a moment and said, "Yes, I don't' think I unloaded it from last year." I then, told him, whatever you do, don't shoot it; it will blow up and possibly kill you or do you some real harm.

I told him that, when we get home, he will have to take his rifle to the local gun shop and the load drawn out before it can be shot again.

I had an afternoon job and I had mornings free to run errands for the gun shop's owner. He would take guns to be repaired to Wilfred Shaw's gun shop in Friendship, Indiana, next to the National Muzzle loading Rifle Association of which he was a long time member.

Wilfred was a retired railroader and a real character that passed on many years ago. It's a real shame when

Life as I Lived It

craftsmen like Wilfred pass on, because they take their trade with them and there's no replacement.

I could go to his shop I the morning and be late for work in the afternoon while I was picking up the repaired guns that were there.

One morning I was at Wilfred's shop to make a pick up and I noticed the tempered glass in his wood burning heat stove was shattered. I asked Wilfred what the heck had happened to the stove door glass and he said, "I shot it out."

I didn't expect that answer, so I said, "Well, you got a bulls eye!" Then we had a good laugh about it and when we were done, he proceeded to tell me how it happened to get broken.

He said he was working on a muzzle loading rifle that had a double load in it and he drew out both loads.

To draw a load out of a muzzle loading rifle, you use a rod with a screw shaped tip that you twist and screw into the soft lead rifle ball, getting a grip on it and then you pull the ball out of the barrel and then dump the powder out. Sounds simple doesn't it. Well it can take a pretty strong tug at times to get it started to move. 'So, Wilfred went on to tell me that after he drew two loads out of the rifle barrel he took a torch to the primer hole to burn out any powder left in the barrel. Well guess what? There was a third load still in the barrel and it fired. The rifle ball ricocheted off the concrete floor and through the door glass on the stove!

I didn't dare tell him I knew who's rifle it was.

Richard W. Block

When I saw Bob next, I told him how lucky he was that he didn't get to shoot his rifle during the deer season! It might have been fatal then!

It pays to be extra aware and careful when shooting muzzle loading guns.

Shooters that compete in matches use a special rod to load with. They use a rod with a round wooden ball or a door knob on the end like a handle for protection in case the gun goes off prematurely while loading a hot barrel. The purpose of the ball or knob on the end is to push your hand out of the way instead of shooting the rod through your hand lie an arrow.

There is method to the madness after all.

MY DOG DUKE

When I was a little boy, I went through so many dogs, I couldn't begin to even count them at this point in my life.

I know I had at least a half dozen dogs that were black and were all named Blackie. As soon as something would happen to one, I'd get another to replace him.

It always seemed that almost every dog I ever had as a child, loved to chase cars for some strange reason and always would wind up being "run over", killing them in the process.

I wasn't limited to just black mutts. I had brown ones, mixed colored ones, all kinds and colors and all not for long it seemed.

As a little boy, I must have been a bad influence on my doggies because they were all rotten in behavior!

Then there was Duke. Duke was the only dog among the lot with any sort of pedigree. He was a border collie. Duke was smart and just like all the other dogs before him; he was dedicated to me as his master and was very protective of me as well. No one dared raise a hand to me that Duke wouldn't bite it off!

I had more torn clothes from that dog than I care to mention. If I even got close to the street, he'd grab on to me and pull me back, away from any possible danger.

Duke wasn't a car chaser. Duke had his own form of entertainment, which would be his undoing in the end. Duke loved to help the mailman deliver his mail and at top speed!

Duke would patiently wait around the corner of the house, poised like a bobcat watching for a rabbit. He'd wait until the mailman had put the mail into the mailbox and when he started across the porch, passing the corner of the house where Duke lay waiting the chase began.

No one realized that ole Bobby S., the mailman, could move that fast!

There would be whooping and hollering and mail flying the rest of the way down the street. This was a daily occurrence!

It didn't take Bobby any length of time to complain to my dad.

I was always amazed at the number of people who knew my dad. I guess when your family has lived in a small town for many generations, you can't help but know just about everybody.

Life as I Lived It

So one Saturday my dad was at home relaxing, when mom told him that the mailman was coming and Duke was waiting in ambush around the corner of the house.

Dad rolled up a newspaper and said, "I'm gonna break ole Duke of his mailman chasing or else", and at this, he waited inside the door for the mailman to show up.

Well, ole Bobby hit the porch and saw dad standing there with newspaper in hand on the other side of the screen door. Dad whispered, "just act normal and put the mail in the box, Duke is waiting for you and I'm going to teach ole Duke a lesson".

Well, I never laughed so hard in my life after the action started, because I was rooting for Duke, because he was my dog!

Well here's what happened.

Bobby reached the corner of the house, Duke sprang out for the attack. Dad burst out the screen door with newspaper in hand, stubbing his big toe as he hit the porch. He was barefoot and hadn't had time to put on his shoes.

There was dad, jumping up and down on one foot while holding the other and shouting obscenities while Duke was helping Bobby on down the street in the usual manner.

I remember dad saying, "that's it! I've had enough of this crap. The dog goes"!

A few days later, dad gave Duke away to a man he knew far away. He said he had a farm and Duke would be happy there. I don't know about Duke, but I wasn't happy about it. A couple of years later, my dad took me squirrel hunting. When we pulled up to the farmer's house to park, there came ole Duke, to my surprise!

Duke hadn't forgotten me. He jumped all over me, so glad to see me.

The farmers name was Alvin Schullenberg. He was an elderly man. He told me how Duke was the best dog he ever had. Duke being a border collie was doing what he was meant to do. He would go out and bring the cows in for milking and then herd them back into the fields. He did this twice a day and was an expert at it, so I was told. Duke had found his niche in life and was a great help and companion to the old farmer. I was glad for them both.

After the chores were finished. Duke came into the woods to find me. We left dad to his hunting and Duke and I played the rest of the day.

I was always welcome to come visit and hunt there, which I did for many years until Alvin passed on and the farm changed hands. I never went back after that. That's just the way life is but I still have my fond memories of the people and the places, something I will always have.

Duke died before Alvin did leaving Alvin alone in life. but one of the things, I remember most about Alvin is the doctor told Alvin he couldn't drive anymore, so Alvin rode his tractor everywhere he went, even to the grocery store! That's a farmer for ya!

MY FIRST BICYCLE

I didn't learn to ride a bicycle until I was about nine years old, so I didn't have one until I was ten and Santa brought it at Christmas time.

Of course, by that time in my life, I knew Santa was really good ole dad.

I remember dad asking me, what kind of bike I wanted and I told him that I wanted one you could peddle backwards, meaning it had gears and hand brakes versus the standard plain bicycle that braked when you pushed the peddles backwards to stop.

I never will forget how great that bike was nor every mile and minute I spent riding it. It was a Schwinn Tiger, 1957 model with a three speed internal hub gear shift system. It was a state of the art bike in 1958, which was the year I got it for Christmas.

It was red and white in color with a name plate on the main frame bar that said "Dick".

Richard W. Block

My dad was not a rich man by any means, but he bought me that bike anyway.

It was one of the best things that my dad ever bought for me. I knew it cost a lot of money and that he surely made sacrifices to be able to buy it. It is gestures like this that made me know how much my dad loved me, even though he didn't say it much in so many words.

My dad was my hero, my idol and I looked up to him. I wanted him to be proud of me. That is the way every dad should be looked upon. Too many people, show too little appreciation too late. When loved ones pass on, the opportunity is gone forever, leaving you behind to wish for the rest of your life, that you had taken the time to say the things left unsaid.

I remember dad telling me, in reference to the bike, that anything else I get with wheels, I will buy myself and that was the way it was.

I took very good care of that bike, right up to the time and beyond, that I was able to buy my first car.

Sometimes I wish I still had that bike. I can still picture it in my mind.

Several years after I was driving my own car, I passed that bike on to a needy young man, who had no bike, but wanted one badly. I wonder if dad was watching from above and if he was proud of me.

MY FIRST JOB

It was 1966, I had just graduated from Aurora High School and I was on a ladder, painting my Grandmother's garage, when I was approached by a middle aged man who was unknown to me.

He introduced himself as Melvin F. from Fehrman Printing Company in Aurora and asked me if I was Richard Block. I said, "Yes, that's me I go by Dick instead of Richard most of the time."

He said, "Fehrman Printing was looking to hire someone in the business and would I be interested in working for them?" I asked, "How did you get me name as a prospect?" Melvin said, "they had a list of names from the High School graduating class of students who the school thought might be available, being they weren't known to have enrolled in other schools or colleges in the coming Fall of the year and my name had reached the top of the list of prospects."

I told Melvin that I suppose I could, but I'd like to finish the painting of the garage first .He said, "Okay, but they would really like for me to start right away," which is what I did, the following morning I was to be there at 8 am. to meet the boss and owner, Bill F., who was Melvin's father, to discuss the terms of employment.

It was an eight to five job workday with an hour for lunch, Monday through Friday. There were no other benefits that I was ever aware of. If I would have been injured on the job, I assumed they would take care of any medical expenses. It was never discussed. Besides, I was just a kid out of high school and never gave it any thought. What could happen anyway? I was always a careful person and being injured on the job never entered my mind.

Bill and his wife owned the business. They were sixty plus years old, I'd say. It was a family run print shop. His son, Melvin ran a linotype machine, which produces lines of lead letters for printing purposes. Bill's son-in-law George M. ran letter presses and set type.

Raymond B. for the most part, was the main man in the shop, who had worked with Bill forever it seems and knew everything there was to know about the printing business and life in general, so I would soon learn. Raymond' daughter, Jackie worked in the front office with Madonna Long, an also long time paper worker who was up in her years as well. Another older woman, Mrs. Hill, ran a linotype machine as well.

Did I say paper worker before? Yes, Bill had owned the local newspaper for ears and had sold it to another newspaper printer in the neighboring town of Lawrenceburg. It was family owned as well. His name was Bill M., a heck of a nice man, I would discover.

Life as I Lived It

Bill F., kept his shop and printed everything else but newspaper. He did, however, print some sections of the newspaper for the newspapers owned by Bill M. in Lawrenceburg.

Bill, my boss, asked me if a dollar per hour wage would be acceptable or if I would prefer a $1.25 per hour wage. I immediately chose the $1.25 per hour wage, while wondering what a silly question that was! Of course I'd prefer $1.25 over only $1.00. Who wouldn't?

With a lot of time, practice and patience, I learned the printing trade from A to Z.

I was what was known as a "printer's devil", which is the same difference as an apprentice in "printer's lingo".

Everyone in the shop constantly drank coffee (known as a cup of mud) and smoked cigars. You were either, filthy dirty from the ink or spotlessly clean handling the paper. There was no in between!

One of the many things I learned was to always be aware of where your hands are at all times. If one of those letter presses caught you off guard it would crush your hands flatter than a pancake while shredding them to pieces with the lead type as the jaws opened and closed during its printing cycle.

I learned to read upside down and backwards as I set or filed type.

Richard W. Block

That's where the phrase "Mind your P's and Q's came from. A lowered case "q" looks like a 'R" when it's set in type. When it's printed on a piece of paper, it's reversed of course, so you had to be careful not to get them mixed up.

You got used to looking at the back side of a print more often than the front, because you were constantly looking to see how hard the press was hitting the paper with the type.

It had to be just so, or you would mash your type and distort the printing.

You don't think about it, but the texture of the ink you use on a printing press is about the same texture as tar.

You put it on the plate with a putty knife and the soft gum rollers spread it out and over the type as the press runs it cycle.

Bill would always check the printing on every job. He never seemed to be satisfied with anything. He was the grumpiest old man I ever saw. He always had a cigar in one hand and a cup of coffee in the other. I can still see him in my mind, shaking his head a mumbling, "Boy, oh boy, oh boy," as he looked over a print. That was always his favorite phrase. I can hear his voice still saying that boy, oh boy, oh boy over and over. I used to mock him when he was out of hearing range on that phrase.

When the 5 P.M. quitting time rolled around, I was gone, and right on the dot too!

Life as I Lived It

That must have made some kind of impression on old Bill because he approached me one day at work and said, "I 've noticed that when the clock strikes 5 p.m. quitting time, you're out of her!" I looked at him with a puzzled look, I'm sure, because I thought quitting time was when you were supposed to stop working and go home!

He glared at me and said, "You're a damn clock watcher, that's what you are. A damn clock watcher!" Then he walked on, leaving me standing there in wonderment.

I thought to myself, old Bill must be under some sort of pressure. There was always plenty of work to be done and we were always hustling to meet deadlines, so, what the heck, I'll stay until 5:30 and leave when they close up for the day.

So I did. I worked until 5:30 every day. After about five or six weeks, Bill called me into his office and asked me, "Why are you working until 5:30 each day instead of 5:00? That is a half hour of overtime; I'm paying you each day extra! Why are you doing that?"

I thought, well darned if I do and darned if I don't! I just can't seem to win! So I looked Old Bill right in the eye and I said with deliberation, "I do it because you need me. There are jobs that need to be finished and if I can get them finished so I can start on another one tomorrow and not have to pick up where I left off the day before. I'd say the progress we are making should speak for itself."

Bill just looked at me and puffed on that big black Ibold cigar of his. I could see that my answer hit him where he lived. He nodded and said, "Okay, you can stay until 5:30."

He was a hard man to understand, but I knew that maybe someday, I'll figure him out.

I always thought Bill hated me until the day came, that I was sitting on a stool minding my own business, filing type away and Bill came walking down the adjacent aisle way. As he passed the end of the aisle I was sitting in, he tripped on a stool and the stool went flying. He stopped in his tracks and looked down the aisle at me and said in his usual grumpy voice, "What did you do that for!" Then he shuffled on down the aisle and was gone.

It was at that very instant everything clicked, I had him figured out!

I grew up among old folks and I'd seen everything when it came to personalities and now I knew what Bill was all about. He was one of those kinds of people who always laughed inside, in his own way, and didn't show it on the outside. He was one of the straight faced types of people.

I'll bet he kicked that stool on purpose just to see the look on my face! That was funny to him. He probably laughed all the way down the aisle and never cracked a smile!

From that point on in time, we were best of friends. I quit avoiding him and went out of my way to get into his way and "pull his chain". I had him figured out and he knew it. We worked as a team and everything was great.

I came into work one day and was informed that Bill had had a stroke and was in the hospital and no one knew any amore about the situation. I went up to the hospital to

Life as I Lived It

see just what was going on and maybe raise the old boy's spirits a little. He was in a very guarded condition and they were allowing no visitors.

I was use do this though, from the many times I had visited the old folks I grew up with in my neighborhood, at the hospital, as they died away, so I knew all the ropes on how to get away with anything I pleased when it came to hospital red tape.

I went up to Bill's room. Some of the family was standing vigil in the hallway I went in to see Bill. All my fears were confirmed the instant I saw his face. I had seen this look before on the faces of others; it was the face of death. I knew he would be gone within 24 hours. It was a sad occasion. I said nothing as I passed his family in the hall.

The next day at work, Raymond asked me how things at the hospital were. I told him that Bill would not be coming home anymore. Raymond understood.

It was like the end of the poem, "There's no joy in Mudville tonight, and the Mighty Casey has struck out."

If you had an Aunt and her name was Emma, chances are you would call her Aunt Em for short.

Well, in the printing business, you used a unit of measure referred to as em's. For example: the columns of print in a newspaper are 12 em's wide. The em's are actually two M.M.'S which means millimeters.

Richard W. Block

Back in 1966, the metric systems meant virtually nothing in the U.S.A. but in the printing business, the metric system had been in use at least a hundred years and more.

We had an instrument called a line guide. It was like a foot long metal ruler. It was squared on one end and rounded on the other. The rounded end was a little larger than the width of the ruler, creating a notch on each side, kind of like a flattened round head bolt would look like.

The line guide was an important instrument. Whenever you set type, you used a type setting tray and a line guide. You set your type right up against the line guide to make sure you didn't make your type too long to fit in whatever designated place it was supposed to go. You had spacers too, to fill in the voids. These were tins, leads and slugs, the tins being the thinnest and slugs being the thickest. The strips of lead from the linotype machines, which had made lettering on them, were called slugs as well.

The linotype machine was a huge piece of equipment with a keyboard just like a typewriter. The only difference was is that it typed out letters in reverse and in lead for printing purposes. It melted and formed the lead into lettering.

One of my duties was to gather all of the used lead from the linotype printings and melt it down in the melting room. There was a huge cast iron pot which sat over a big gas burner about knee high into which I dumped all the lead slugs that we were finished using and melted them down.

Once the lead was molten, I added a black soot type substance call "Inksolve", which brought all of the

Life as I Lived It

impurities to the top of the molten lead and then I would skim it off with a skimmer which was made of cast iron.

Once the lead was melted and cleaned, it was ready to do one of two things with, poured into pigs or into cuts.

A pig is shaped like a boat. It's about 3 inches wide at the top, 3 inches deep at the bottom and about 3 feet long, pointed at one end and flat with an eyelet for hanging on the other. This is what the linotype machine used. The pig hung on a chain and was lowered into a melting pot on the linotype as was needed when it was printing out slugs. We had 6 pig molds made of cast iron.

This is the process that caused me to start wearing western style boots instead of the low cut Hush Puppies that I wore all of my life up to this point.

I'd put on my heavy gloves and pick up the big cast iron ladle and start to dip it into the pot of molten lead very, very, slowly, letting the ladle heat up to the temperature of the lead. It would snap, crackle and pop as I did this, reminding me that if I tried to just stick that cold ladle into the hot molten lead to quickly, it would cause an explosion! Once the ladle was heated you could dip the molten lead just as if dipping water..

It was at this point in the process that you had to contend with the cold cast iron pig molds. There was no way to heat them up other than just pouring the molten lead into them and when I did this the lead would spatter out of the cold mound and land on my shoes and socks where it would burn my ankles. I learned to just stand there grit my teeth and take the hits.

If I danced around, I'd naturally spatter more from the hot ladle and on to myself! It was this factor that motivated me to wear boots and shield my ankles!

Now the cuts were a different kind of pouring process.

You had what was called a "Matt", which was a heavy fiber type of cardboard like material with pictures and/or advertisements imprinted into its surface. I'd frame the matt in place, creating a mold and then pour the molten lead into the mold. When the lead hardened and you removed the framework and matt, you were left with what was called a cut. I'd then trim the cut to the needed size on a table saw and then I put it on the router to cut out any high spots that might leave a shadowy imprint on the paper while being printed. In this manner you were highlighting what was to be printed and recessing anything that might cause a problem. This took craftsmanship and I enjoyed being one of the best in the business when I created the cuts for the newspaper adds.

As time went on I moved to other jobs with other companies and other occupations.

And of course most of these people have all passed on and the company as well as the building that housed it, does not exist anymore.

When I think back about the six years I spent working there, I recall that I never received a raise in pay not even

Life as I Lived It

once in that length of time. As long as one is doing a job that one enjoys, sometimes the money aspect is not much of a factor.

As long as I could pay my bills and afford gas and ammo and have a few dollars left over between paydays, I had no complaints!!

That's the way life should be. Don't you agree?

MY RIFLE

In 1958, when I was ten years old, my Dad bought me my first rifle. It was a .22 caliber, model 67 Winchester youth model, bolt action, single shot rifle. It was beautiful, well, to me anyway. I killed my first squirrel with it.

When I turned 12, my Dad bought me a .20 gauge shotgun. It was a Winchester, model 37, youth model, single shot. I thought it was beautiful too and I still have it.

It was soon after I got the shotgun that my Dad asked me if it was okay if he could give my rifle to his brother Lloyd (my uncle) for his son to keep and learn to shoot with. Well, I couldn't very well refuse him, now that I have the new shotgun, so away it went, never to be seen again.

Down deep, I suppose I always regretted giving up the rifle. I think I always wanted it back because it was my first rifle, a gift from my Father.

So, a couple of years before my Uncle passed on, I asked him what ever happened to the little rifle he got from my Dad and he told me he had given it to his ex-son-in-law,

Life as I Lived It

whom I knew still lived in the area after leaving the family through divorce.

While my Uncle had the rifle, he had a telescope sight added to the rifle. This I knew, because my Father told me about it soon after it was given to my Uncle.

One day I had the opportunity to talk to Butch, the ex-son-in-law and I asked him if he still had the rifle he got from his ex-father-in-law and he said no. I asked, "Well, what happened to it?" Butch told me he sold it long ago. I asked, "To whom?" He told me it was so many years ago that he didn't know anymore.

Well, that was the end of that. I guess it is a lost cause. I will never get it back.

I had wound-up about 30 miles from my little hometown of Aurora as the years went by.

I bought some land and built a house near Milan, Indiana, the little town that won the State Basketball Championship in 1954. They made a movie named "Hoosiers" about it.

My neighbor Ralph likes to buy or sell things that other neighbors or friends bring to him.

Sometimes he will call me and ask me the value of things, especially guns.

One day, Ralph called me and wanted to know the value of a .22 rifle someone had brought to him to sell. He said it was sitting in his bedroom and to come take a look at it, even though he wouldn't be home.

So, when I was near his home, I thought I ought to stop in and see what he has this time.

He was not home, so I let myself in and went into his bedroom to see the rifle, so I could give him an idea of its value. I looked around and finally spotted the rifle in the corner of the half dark room. I picked it up and walked out into the light where I could take a better look at it and to my surprise, it was MY rifle!

I called Ralph on his cell phone and when he answered, I said, "Where did you get my rifle?"

He said, "Your rifle!!" I said, "Yes, my rifle!" "I have been looking for this gun for 50 years and here it is!" Ralph told me that a man over in a neighboring town had died and his wife was selling some of his possessions through a neighbor friend of hers.

I said to Ralph, "I am leaving a hundred dollar bill on the table and I am taking the gun with me." It was a fair price I felt. Besides, there were still specks of white paint on the stock from when my Mother painted the bedroom woodwork when I was young.

I took the little rifle home and took the telescope sight and base off the rifle. Whoever mounted that on the rifle, did a very poor job. The scope and mount were cock-eyed on the rifle. It did not look down the barrel, but off to one side.

Life as I Lived It

I took the rifle to the gun show in Indianapolis, where I have a gun parts friend and showed him the rifle. His name is Butch and he gasped while asking, "Who in their right mind would drill holes in a rifle like this?" I replied, "It wasn't me! I just want to plug the mount holes."

Butch, being the guru of gun parts, found four plug screws with the right thread and filled the holes.

It is not perfect but it is close enough and whenever I look at it, I can see my Father's love radiating from it.

MY SECRET HUNTS

I am going to tell you about a sport hunting that I like to do. It is a challenging hunt that keeps me on my toes in a different sense of meaning.

I carefully plan my hunts. I scope out the best areas and the best time of the day to hunt them. Sometimes I use maps and sometimes I just go by the lay of the land.

The best hunting areas are always the densest of underbrush and/ or swamp.

Places with small ponds of water or lakes are pretty good hunting as well.

You have to be very quiet as you make your way through the underbrush. You want to be as unnoticeable as possible, trying to be as invisible as you can while you are hunting.

The good thing is, is that there is no limit on how many you take home. Also, there is a long season which never closes in some states. Sometimes I will get as many as fifty!

Life as I Lived It

But, then the work begins. Sometimes it takes more time than you want to spend just to clean them all. But I think it is worth it.

People are always asking me, "How many did you get today?" Hell, I don't mind bragging a little, so I tell them straight out! "I got plenty this morning!" A lot of folks are just plain amazed. They ask, "How do you get so many?"

I tell them you just have to be a hunter at heart. You have to be determined and willing to hunt in areas where no one else dare to venture. You have to be very focused on your prey, any little hump in the leaves; any little patch of color that is out of place could give their hunting place away. You have to look especially in low places, under tree, roots, dense growth, bushes that are thick, tall grass, edges of water holes and sometimes just out in the wide open.

It seems like you find them when you least expect and more often than not!

What am I hunting you keep wondering?

Golf balls of course!!!

MY SON BUBBIE

How old was I when Bubbie came to me, it seems like only yesterday. His mother had suffered an untimely death and I was alone raising four children and now a fifth. Bubbie was such a bundle of joy, feeding him his bottle and holding him while he slept. He was such a tiny thing.

His brothers and sister were a few years older than Bubbie, but he was welcomed with open arms. I explained to them that their little brother must be given their full attention and loving care and must never be left alone. Bubbie spent every night sleeping with one of his brothers, Mike or Robbie taking turns most of the time and Dad too.

He only cried when he was hungry and he was so very active with his enormous curiosity of life's little perks. He was always opening doors ad drawers and sorting through every little item. Then along came the discovery of Hot Wheels, a whole box full of the small cars that his brother Mike kept in the bathroom, another pick up project for ole Dad.

As Bubbie grew he learned about telephones, TV. remotes and then – Nintendo video games. His lightning speed on the controller drove his brother crazy with envy.

Life as I Lived It

His sister Kelly had married and had a son Tyler. Now he was Uncle Bubbie! His oldest brother Richard was appointed to the United Stated Military Academy at West Point and was away for most of the time, coming home only on major holidays and a couple of weeks in the summer. I think Richard's relationship with Bubbie suffered a lot because of his long absence.

Bubbie's high I.Q. enabled him to learn a good understanding of a foreign language. Bubbie loves the Boy Scouts and the games they play and swimming too. Then I taught Bubbie about animals especially dogs and he learned about guns, what makes them work and that pulling the trigger makes the gun go boom!!

The foreign language Bubbie learned to understand is English and if you haven't figured it out yet, he is a RACCOON!!

A photograph of Bubbie and his brother Richard was posted at West Point showing them on the sofa together, paging through a logistics book. Cadets used to write him letters and I would respond to them for him. I still get invites to gun shows in the mail addressed to Bubba Block.

NATURE'S LITTLE LESSONS

It was a typical early fall day in September and I was headed for the woods on one of my neighbor's farms to do some squirrel hunting and perhaps a little scouting around for the upcoming deer season in October.

I was still hunting along the edge of a cow pasture which was more brush and briars than grass which bordered a corn field.

I grew up around cattle and I always enjoyed hunting in areas where cattle roamed because the other animals were used to their activity and they made paths that both man and beast made use of in their travels.

Still hunting is the art of moving around as you hunt. The rule is, you take a step, then you take a look, and you do more looking than stepping. In this manner, the animal sneaks up on you rather than you on them.

I was just about to the edge of the woods when I saw him, coming down the same path I was on, without a care in the world. It was a groundhog (woodchuck) and he was getting closer with each waddling step. You know, you don't have to shoot something just because the opportunity presents itself. Sometimes there's a meaning of greater value.

I slowly spread my feet as I stood motionless. Let's see if he passes through I thought. He stopped short of my toe and slowly looked up, following my features like a child at the base of the Statue of Liberty.

Then he went around me and into the closest bramble bushes where I saw him pick something bulb like and eat it before moving on. I slipped into the bramble to find a pear tree that even the lifelong landowner never knew was there. The ground was full of deer tracks. The deer liked eating the pears also.

When I returned to the owner's home, I told him about the pear tree. He was stunned and went to see it for his self to believe it was there. For years after, we killed deer in the area of that tree and owed it all to the ground hog that showed it to us.

NEIGHBORHOOD GROCERY

I'm sure that somewhere in everyone's lifetime they had shopped at a neighborhood grocery store. You know what I mean. It's the little store just down the street that carries the bare necessities, the basic needs that saves you from having to go to the large supermarket farther away.

These little "mom and pop" owned stores are becoming fewer and fewer, giving way to what is known as convenience stores, connected with gas stations. The "one stop shop" is the common phrase they used. Heck, you don't even know who owns them! In the old neighborhood grocery, everyone knew who they were. They were part of the neighborhood. They lived upstairs, in the rear or next door to their little place of business. You called them by name and they did you the same. Everyone knew everyone, like one big family.

The neighborhood I grew up in was no exception. Bud and Mary C. operated the little grocery at the bottom of our street.

I was a familiar face there, just like everyone else that lived nearby. My mom was always sending me there to

Life as I Lived It

get something she needed. I had a "Radio" scooter with a basket on the front that was just the right size to hold a six bottle carton of RC Cola.

I remember one time, I was busy playing or something and she wanted me to stop what I was doing and go to the store. I replied, "Why do I always have to go?" I still remember her answer as if it was only yesterday. She said, "Well! What do you think I have you for?" "So, I don't have to go to the store".

I really didn't mind going, I just like to fuss about it to see if it made any difference and guess what, and it didn't.

There was, however, one time each month that I hated to go to the store for Mom's needs. It was the dreaded trip to buy the box of Kotex sanitary napkins. Every time I'd sit that box on the counter, Millie, the lady who worked there for the owners, would tease me something awful. It was embarrassing to me, to say the least! She would say loud enough for everyone in the store to hear, "Well! What are you going to do with those?" I'd turn red, say nothing, and pay the money and leave. This procedure was getting to be pretty old and I was darn tired of being embarrassed in front of everyone, every time I made that trip.

So, one day, I was on my way to the store and I had decided that there would be no more embarrassment. This time, I am going to reverse the situation. This time I'm going to "get her goat!" So I thought. I need an answer that's halfway believable and totally unexpected. To make a long story short, I sat that box of napkins on the counter along with the money. She made her usual expected remark.

235

Richard W. Block

"Well! What are you going to do with those?" I spoke right up for everyone to hear. I said, in a matter of fact manner, "I use these to clean my shotgun. They just fit a .12 gauge. I thought everyone knew that."

She had this look of bewilderment on her face and for once, she had no idea of what to say in reply. She handed me my change, I grabbed the box and left everyone standing there, wondering about what I had just said. Hell, I got everybody's goat that time!

I patted myself on the back all the way home! A month later, I find myself making the trip again to the store for the box of sanitary napkins and wondering along the way, what the result will be this time.

I sat the box on the counter in anticipation of Millie's comment. She looked down at me and said, "Cleaning the shotgun again, hugh?"

I said, "Yep, you betchya!" As I walked home with the box under my arm, it occurred to me that "cleaning the shotgun" may have taken a whole new meaning!

Many years have passed now and the people as well as the buildings haven't existed for some time, but the memories still linger where vacate lots lie.

NEW YEAR'S BLAST

Living in a small town environment has its advantages as well as its traditions and one of these traditions is on New Year's Eve.

As the ball drops on Times Square on TV, most folks step outside with gun in hand to shoot into the air and cheer in the New Year as the zero hour chimes. I've always enjoyed this practice as well as listening to others do the same as far away as can be heard.

So, I was skeptical to say the least when I moved to a new neighborhood in a town fifteen miles away. However, I breathed a sigh of relief when I discovered everyone in the neighborhood had target ranges behind their houses that got frequent use.

I kept a low profile that first New Year's Eve. I wanted to see how they celebrated the zero hour. To my delight, no worries, it's just like home! People cheering, singing, shooting into the air, what a party!!

My Cousin Jimmie James and I were black powder enthusiasts and built our own cannons. I'd built two of the finest pirate deck guns you'd ever wanted to see. "Next Year", I'm thinking, "I'll throw a surprise party for the neighbors!!!"

Now its next year and zero hour is approaching, I rolled the two cannons from my garage into the darkness of my driveway, turning them ninety degrees facing down the row of house fronts, loaded and primed ready for action.. Just seconds before the zero hour, I lit the fuse on no. 1 gun. The whole neighborhood appeared as expected and as the clock struck, so did no. 1 with its tremendous boom and blast of fire recoiling backward as I lit no. 2 with the same result.

When the smoke cleared, everyone had gone. The surprise was on me!! The celebration was instantly over and everyone was afraid to come out. I had no idea it would spoil all the fun. I felt bad about it and didn't do it anymore in the years to come, but neither did the whole neighborhood. It was a joke gone wrong on my part!

OZZIE

When I was a kid, the five and dime store sold baby chicks at Easter time.

They were dyed three different colors, red, blue and green and they were all rooster chicks.

After they grew bigger, the colors would naturally fade away and they would be white in color.

My cousin Jimmy lived three houses down the street from me. He was two years older than me and we did everything together.

Naturally when Easter time came, we would get a colored chick to raise as a pet.

They were always so cute and we played with them until they got too big to be any fun to play with anymore

My Dad always took my sister's and my chickens to our cousin's farm in the next town and put them in with their chickens when they matured. Jimmy kept his a little longer and you could hear him crowing frequently every day.

Richard W. Block

Jimmy named him Ozzie and he grew to be pretty big. He was fun to chase around and try to catch, he was fast.

One day, Jimmy's Dad decided it was time to invite Ozzie in for dinner, so he cut his head off with an ax and plucked him for the dinner feast. Jimmy was heartbroken.

He wouldn't eat his dinner because he knew it was Ozzie on his plate.

The next day Jimmy was eating a sandwich his mother fixed for him at lunch time. He made the remark that "Gee this is really good mom, what is it?" Upon hearing that, she said, "Ozzie salad of course!"

And now, my poem.
Jimmy's daddy took an ax
And gave poor Ozzie a couple whacks.
Then he plucked him just for fun
and fed him to his only son.
It was such a dreadful sight,
But he tasted good, to the very last bite!
Poor Ozzie.....

PAW PAW TREE

One of my job duties was to mow my seventy plus year old boss's grass.

His lawn was on a grad for the most part and very few flat areas with trees of all sizes to mow around.

I didn't like the mount of trimming I had to do around all those trees. They were a bunch of obstacles to me to have to content with when I mowed.

There was this one paw paw tree that stood alone in a remote area of the yard that was about twenty feet tall with only one limb at the top and about as big as a grapefruit at the base. It was not a tree of any worth or beauty, so I thought it would be better off, being gone.

So I got a shovel and ax and proceeded to remove it. I didn't want any trace of the tree to be left, so I dug around the base to find the main tree roots and the cut them with the ax. Once that was done, I just pushed the tree over.

That way, there is no telltale stump left in the ground. Then I peeled the grass sod back and skimmed the bare ground for some fill dirt to fill the hole and level out the hump the tree makes as it grows, pushing the dirt up with its roots. Then I rolled the sod back into place so you couldn't tell there was anything ever there. I lopped the tree into several pieces and put it back into the woods to rot.

It was never missed and it was one less thing to mow around.

A couple of years later, the boss and I were walking around the yard in the area of the old paw paw tree and he stopped and looked around for a time and asked, "Wasn't there a paw paw tree in this area?"

I looked around too, just to play along and said, "No I don't think so." "I don't see a stump or anything." Besides there were still several paw paw trees along the upper edge of his yard against the edge of the woods.

So, the conversation turned to something else and the tree thought was dismissed.

About a year late, there was a maple tree that had died and needed to be taken down. It was a stocky tree about fifteen inches in diameter and pretty tall as well. The boss looked at it and remarked it needed to be cut down and he was determined that he was going to help. I knew from previous experiences, that if he helped it was going to take twice as long to get the job done.

I knew his intentions were good and I loved the old guy too, even though we would butt heads on occasions, we were still great friends.

Life as I Lived It

We went to the garage for some tools. I got the shovel and ax and he showed up with the chain saw. I asked him, "What are you going to do with that?" He replied, "I am going to cut the tree down." I said, "Oh, no you're not!" "Just stand back and watch how I do it so there is no stump left to contend with."

So I dug around the tree to reveal the main roots and then severed them with the ax. Then I said, "Come and help me give the tree a little push." At that, the tree fell over and rolled out of place. I rolled the sod back and skimmed the top soil to smooth out the hump and fill the hole. Then I rolled the sod back and it looked as though the tree was never there!

I said, "Now, we can use the chain saw". He said, "So this is what happened to the missing paw paw tree". I had to laugh and said, "Yes, I just can't get away with nothing around here!" At that, we both laughed about it.

PETE

Pete Z. was our next door neighbor at work. He was a dentist and his building joined our little manufacturing company on Main Street in Lawrenceburg, Indiana.

Our building bordered an alley with a vacant gravel lot which was owned by a flooring Company across the street.

Everyone hated Pete because he would just barge in and go up the stairs to the office and yell, complaining about the few parking spaces out front on the street were always occupied by some of your workers cars that sat there all day and his patients had no place to park! I didn't dislike him because I could see his point of view and I didn't blame him for being a jackass about it, so I decided to make a friend out of him. So I went out of my way to change his disposition and win him over.

A long time ago, I read a book by Dale Carnegie Its title is, "How to Win Friends and Influence people". I recommend it to everyone to read. I always gave a copy to each of our salesmen to read. It really improved their salesmanship. I

I enjoyed Dale's book and I couldn't put it down once I started reading it.

I learned long ago that when you know the shit is going to hit the fan, attack first.

There's nothing like the element of surprise.

Every time I would see Pete, I would say Hi and ask how things are going for him and the parking situation. Sometimes I had to go out of my way to do it. When I saw him at other places of business I would always acknowledge him. After a month or two, Pete got down right friendly and he never came in our building, making a scene again.

Why is it human nature for people to make someone out to be a villain of sort, when they are really not a bad person at all?

PINTO PANIC

My partner Clyde and his wife, Betty, were going away on vacation. They had a dog. It was one of those feisty little terriers. You neither know the kind that never sits still nor stop yapping all the time. He always boarded his dog in a kennel which, at that time, cost about $30.00 a week. So, I offered to keep his dog and save him some money.

Besides, where is the fun in being cooped up in a kennel with strangers, when you look at it from the dog's point of view of course?

My wife and two children accompanied me when I picked the dog up at Clyde's house. The road home passed through Mt. Airy Forest. As I drove along, I noticed something lying in the road ahead on the center line. I stopped alongside of the object and opened my door to discover a fresh hit gray squirrel that wasn't there when I passed through before.

I laid the squirrel on the floor of my little Ford Pinto beside my seat and drove on thinking of the fried squirrel I'd be having for supper tonight. Thirty miles later, I stopped at the grocery for some milk. As I walked to the grocery, I heard my family yelling and screaming. I ran back to the

Life as I Lived It

car and this is what I saw through the window. Apparently the slamming of the car door awoke the stunned and not dead gray squirrel, who was now doing laps around the inside of my small car with a dog hot on his tail, jumping from front seat to back seat across the legs and laps of three screaming people who were begging for rescue. I opened the door just long enough for the squirrel to escape and keep the dog inside.

Oh well, easy come – easy go. No squirrel tonight, but boy what an exit!!!..When I came out of the store, an observer who saw the whole thing said, "Your pet squirrel is under that car over there", while pointing a finger. I said, "That's no pet, that's a hitchhiker!"

RABBIT

I was on my way to work one morning and I had just left the farm when a rabbit ran out from the roadside weeds and hit the side of my wheel. I looked in my mirror and I could see him lying in the road. I backed up and opened my door.

He looked like there wasn't a mark on him, so I picked him up and put him on the floor mat. Why leave a perfectly good rabbit lying in the road for the buzzards, when I can have him for my supper so on to work I went

I worked for a small company in Lawrenceburg with a bunch of women coworkers. When break time came around I got the rabbit from my car and skinned it outside behind our building where the dumpsters were and no one could see what I was doing. I cut the rabbit up into frying pieces and put them in a bowl of salt water in the break area refrigerator.

When quitting time rolled around, I took my rabbit home and had myself a nice fried rabbit supper. It was great.

Life as I Lived It

The next day at work, the whole place was in an up roar. To hear all those women coworkers tell it, you would have thought that I had personally crucified Jesus Christ himself and cut him up getting blood all over the place and creating some gruesome scene at the workplace for all to see!

The owners were upset and the management was beside themselves over the situation.

What a bunch of crybabies. They always could make a mountain out of a mole hill.

RADIOS

I was driving somewhere on a trip. I always have a C.B. radio in use each time I go anywhere. I like to keep track of where the cops are, traffic problems and weather conditions and so on.

"C.B. radios are the windows to the world,'" is what I tell everyone who asks me how can I stand to listen to that entire racket that comes from the radio?

I've been into CB radios since 1966, when my Uncle Leonard, my mom's brother, got me interested in them.

I remember when they were all tubes instead of transistors and they were five times the size of what they are now.

I started out with a base station, as was customary.

My F.C.C. license call sign was KRK-2354. My Uncles was KPJ-8988. I used to talk to my cousin Jimmy daily. You were limited to a 150 mile range and in those days, it was easy to talk farther then the limit allowed.

Life as I Lived It

The Federal Communications Commission, known as Uncle Charlie, kept pretty close watch over the airwaves. Idle chit chat, foul language and excessive use, were offenses which could cause you to lose your license and equipment.

The F.C.C. had locator trucks that could cross reference your transmissions and pinpoint your location and they were very serious about it too!

I know avid radio operators who received warning tickets from the F.C.C. and up and sold their equipment, just to keep from being fined and jailed in the future.

Linear amplifiers were also illegal, but I had one and used it sparingly. You were allowed five watts maximum output by law. I had an 80 watt linear, which gave me 80 watts of output.

Once in a while you would run across radio operators who continually broke the rules and were a nuisance and this is where they were taught a lesson.

Every time they were being a nuisance, all you had to do was transmit at the same time as they did, except with the linear turned on. This wiped out their transmission. Your 80 watts of power would wipe out their 5 watt transmission! Whoever they would be talking to would hear nothing but silence. They would hear him start to talk, but be blotted out by a more powerful signal. This was known as throwing a carrier. A carrier is a transmission with no sound.

After a while of not being able to talk to anyone else on their radio, the person being the nuisance develops manners.

Things are so different now. The F.C.C. deregulated the C.B. range. No License is required. Everyone abuses the usage. Foul language runs rampant. People have no consideration for anything or anyone. Racial slurs and bad jokes are frequent as well, so you have to be careful when using it around children.

One great benefit I have always enjoyed is that it is great at keeping me awake, especially when I'm driving all night long to get somewhere.

Shooting the breeze with truck drivers going the same direction, makes the hours go away at

an amazing rate. Plus it is educational in many ways. You learn something from everyone you talk to.

I've met many people from all over the world on those radios and made many friends as well, and by friends, I mean people, whom I met face to face and became part of each other families! Lifelong friends!

A funny story, I was listening to a couple of truckers talking on the radio. The one trucker was telling the other about an incident that happened the week before, when he was running along with another truck driver reroute to somewhere. They decided they would stop at a McDonald's and get some food and drink to go and eat it as they moved on down the road, because time was short.

Life as I Lived It

His buddy in the other truck just wanted a Coke and a plain quarter pounder with cheese. They got their food and were headed on down the road a few miles, when his buddy discovered that his quarter pounder with cheese was dressed normal, with the catsup, mustard, pickle and onion, instead of plain.

Well, it wasn't worth the trouble to take it back at this point, so he decided to just remove the top of the bun with all the condiments on it and eat it like that. He rolled down his window a piece and threw the bun top out the window, rather than leave it lay around in the truck.

The next thing you know, there's a police car with his lights flashing, demanding he pull over, which he did in compliance.

His buddy watched the policeman in his mirror as he approached the cab of his truck and rolled down his window at the same time. The policeman saw him watching and motioned him to come down and follow him to the rear of the truck.

As they reached the rear end, the policeman pointed to the windshield of his cruiser. There, in the center of his windshield, was the quarter pounder bun top, held firmly in place by the catsup, mustard, pickle and onion like a fine glue.

His buddy just said nothing and headed back to the truck cab. The policeman said, "where do you think you're going?' His buddy replied, "I'm going to get my Windex and some paper towels so I can clean your windshield."

After all was in order, the policeman remarked, "I'm not going to give you a ticket because the bun is a food source and not considered actual litter, but I would like an honest answer to this question. Did you see me start to pass and throw the bun on purpose, or was it just a case of bad timing?"

To this, his buddy replied, "I didn't even know you were behind me, I just tossed it at random, it wasn't intentional, and I assure you!"

I'm sure he told the truth, but it does leave a lot of room for speculation!

It's funny. You talk to someone often, whom you've never seen and you form an image of how they must look by the sound of their voice and the manner of their personality and when you do finally meet face to face, they are nothing close to what you had pictured them to be! I learned to picture them in the opposite manner after a while and found I was closer to reality more often than not.

One of my dearest friends, I met over the radio. His name was Larry Wyatt and he lived in Lawrenceburg, which was five miles from my base station. We talked daily.

He told me that he was always home and to call anytime. So I did and he was always there to answer. Every time I passed through town, I'd call from my car mobile and we would talk all the way home. His handle was Green Slime. Some handle huh?

Life as I Lived It

He gave me directions to his house and I decided one day that I was just going to have to meet this character, I mean, how can someone always be home and always on his radio?

Well, this was one of those true to form experiences, where the person was nothing like I had visualized.

I was overwhelmed by the friendly greeting I received from Larry's parents. They invited me in and pointed me in the right direction saying, "Go on in, Larry's in the front room and he'll be glad to finally meet you!"

I went in and I was shocked. Larry's room consisted of a bed, a few chairs, a hospital table that held his radio equipment and an iron lung, in which he slept at night.

Larry was two years older than I and had polio when he was about 6 or 7 years old. His two younger brothers, Lanny and Lenny had suffered from it as well, but it did not do the damage that it did to Larry.

Larry was totally bed ridden and could only move his head and had the use of his right arm and hand, with which he could key his D-104 lollypop mike to talk on his radio.

After we shook hands and started talking, his situation made no difference.

You see, Larry was a survivor. He had a great personality that didn't get him down. We became fast friends and I was "adopted' into their family, as were other people like myself.

Larry's brother Lanny was my age. We would load Larry up in their family station wagon and go to the dump and shoot our pistols.

I used to tease Larry that one day; he was going to shoot his big toe off because he had to shoot from a laying position. He never did though, because he was a pretty good shot in spite of his handicap!

Larry lived to his mid-forties before passing on.

My parents are gone but I still have his, which I call Mom and Dad as well.

I rarely pass through Lawrenceburg that I don't think of the identifying "ping" sound of his Browning Eagle radio when it began to transmit. I miss it.

I remember telling Frank S., (an old scouter), at his wife's funeral in an attempt to give him peace of mind that, "They're never really gone, as long as they're remembered by those who knew them." One of my better quotes!!

RANDOM EXPRESSIONS

I have compiled a list of expressions that people don't say much anymore or do they still?

I am sure there are some not on my list that you can add to it!

It's a dog day afternoon
Fair to middle'n (a Southern term meaning a grade of cotton)
Deep as a well
Useless as tits on a boar hog
Smells like death warmed over
Little miss sunshine
Mad as a wet hen
Full of horse puck
Stupid is, as stupid does
He smokes like a chimney
Elbows off the table
Sleep tight
Don't let the bed bugs bite
Where there is smoke, there is fire
Boiling hot
Sharp as a tack

Richard W. Block

Dull as a knife
Beyond help
High as a kite
Queer as a 3 dollar bill
Full of crap
Nose like a blood hound
Eagle beak (nose)
Hollow as a tree
Flat as a pancake
In one ear and out the other
Cool as a cucumber
Hurts like hell
Hot as hell
Sweet as candy
Sour as a grape
Wrinkled like a prune
Slick as snot
Slick as a whistle
Right as rain
Dead wrong
Dead right
Lite as air
Loud mouth
Silly as a clown
Quiet as a mouse
White hot
Mean as a snake
Sweet as honey
Slower than a 7 year itch
Slower than molasses
Fast as lightning
Smokin hot
He has to speed up to stop

Life as I Lived It

That's a doozie
Gee whiz
Quicker than a jack rabbit
Soft as silk
Dumber than a box of rocks
Cold as ice
You dumb bell
White as snow
Black as coal
It's a snap!
Happy as a Lark
Crazy as a loon
Bigger than life
Big as a mountain
Nuttier than a fruit cake
Red as a beet
Scared stiff
Scared yellow
Lickity split!
Green as grass
Bluer than blue
Sky blue
Tears as big as raindrops
Dead as a door nail
Helpless as a newborn baby
Quick as a flash
Add your own to the list.

RAPE

I was sitting in my living room, watching TV and listening to the rain that was pouring down outside.

Somewhere among the sounds of the rain I could hear someone screaming, "Help me! Someone help me, they are trying to rape me!"

I got up and looked out the window and saw this teenage girl running down the middle of the street barefoot in soaking wet clothing, being chased by 5 boys.

People were looking out their windows and turning on their porch lights, but no one was doing anything about it!

By this time, I had moved to the front door and asked my wife to hand me my pistols from the coffee table and to call 911 for the police and have them send someone to our address.

I opened the door and stepped half way out. I yelled to the girl to come over here, which she did instantly with the boys close behind. When she got to the door I pulled her

Life as I Lived It

inside and came up to bear with my pistol as the boys hit the porch.

I yelled, "Stop right there or I'll drop every one of you in the blink of an eye!"

I told them the police were on their way and to stand right where you are and don't move. Within minutes the police arrived and put the boys in their police cars.

I in the meantime had my wife get the girl a bath towel to dry off with. The police talked to her and took her along with them as well.

The next morning my neighbor, Rick, from across the street came over to talk. Rick is one of those Civil War Reenactors. He said he was glad that I did something about the situation last night.. He said those kids would have been 2 blocks down the street by the time he could get his muzzle loader loaded.

I told him that where I come from we don't put up with that crap!

I never did get my bath towel back……

RATS

Late February and March is flood season along the Ohio River. Pool stage is 26 to 27 feet. Flood stage is 52 feet which is even with the highway along the river in Aurora, Indiana.

Anything over 52 feet puts the water over the road and into town, closing off some of the streets. Once this is happening, the water drives the rats and other vermin to higher ground. The next thing you know is they are invading people's homes and you have to do something to be rid of them.

I was still in high school at the time of one of the floods and I was sitting in the living room reading my shop class book, when I saw a rat walking across the floor near the kitchen. I slowly closed my book and stood up while watching to rat snoop around. I took careful aim and threw the book, which hit and killed him. That was a lucky throw.

In another occurrence, there was this really smart and elusive rat that had chewed a hole in the wall, in the kitchen cupboard at ground level. He would come and go anytime he pleased and I just couldn't seem to be able to

Life as I Lived It

catch him. I set all kinds of traps everywhere in the house and he would get the bait and not get caught. Sometimes he would trip the trap and sometimes not, but he always was able to get away without getting caught.

One day, I heard him rummaging around in the kitchen cupboard. I quietly slipped over to the cupboard door and slowly opened it. There he sat, taunting me as if to think to himself, you can't catch me!

Well I had had just about enough of this damn rat, so I pulled out my pistol and shot him dead! I figured a bullet hole in the floor would be a good trade for his demise. I think that was the last time we had a rat problem in our house. Maybe the smell of the rat's blood kept them away.

Oh, I bought my first pistol when I was 16 years old. It was legal then.

REDNECK

What is a Redneck? What defines a Redneck?

What comes to mind when you think of a person that you would call a Redneck?

I think most people think of a Redneck as being some kind of Country bumpkin set in his backwoods ways of manner and dress, that may be a little backwards or slow thinking or moving.

That way of thinking is somewhat off track. Sure it is a person that lives in the country. Who lives in the Country? Farmers of course and farmers spend a great deal of their time working in the field, plowing, discing, planting the seeds, cultivating and harvesting the crops.

Thus, they spend a lot of time in the hot sun, which gives them a red neck from the sun's ultraviolet rays. So, he always has a red neck, thus the term Redneck was derived, referring to the Farmers of America!!

REVERSE PSYCHOLOGY

Doesn't it just drive you crazy when one or more of your children do one of their crying and screaming routines and not matter what you do, they continue on being the center of attention?

They used to, (key words) used to pull that routine on me, their dear old Dad. Until one day, I just snapped.

I have had enough! I thought what the heck; I'll play this game too! So I joined in acting just like the kids!

Then I let them have it, just like a Marine drill sergeant. "What's that? I can't hear you"! You call that crying? You'll have to do better than that! Louder! Louder!! I'd yell "You've got to do better than that! I can't hear you!" "Louder!!"

You'd be surprised how really short a time it takes for a child to wear itself out and quiet down. Oh sure, they will pull their routine again just to see if they can get somewhere with it. And of course, I'd do mine, getting them nowhere.

After a very short period of time, they figured that they were wasting their time on tantrums and never did them again!

That's reverse psychology at its finest!

RICOCHET

The mid 1960's was a time of unrest on the world front. It seemed like everyone you knew was being drafter for the Vietnam War cause.

I was worried to say the least, because all you heard about on TV was the deaths of our soldiers due to the new M-16 rifles jamming and locking up in the middle of a fire fight and finding their bodies with their disassembled weapon in hand!

A close friend of mine, who returned from the thick of it, told me that when my turn comes don't get a M-16 with the open 3 prong muzzle brake, get the newer enclosed one because the 3 prong catches every vine, leaf and weed and you are forever cleaning crap out of the muzzle.

I never did fully trust the M-16 and still don't. I was happy to get my hands on a tommy gun. I was old fashioned and favored older weapons. Give me that .45 cal. With stick mags and I'll show you reliability and knock down power at close range.

Richard W. Block

We were on the range on day and there was a tank sitting there. Just I and two buddies were there. I decided to see what effect my tommy gun would have when the .45 cal slug hit the steel. I knew it wouldn't hurt the tank; I just wanted to see what the slugs would do. I leveled my weapon and looked down the sights. An odd feeling hit me with the message of bounce back or ricochet. I lowered my weapon and thought, no, what are the odds of being hit? Oh, like winning the lottery, right? I leveled again, looking through the sights and again the same feeling.

I squeezed the trigger and I can still see in my mind, that .45 cal slug, smacking that tank and coming straight back at me, hitting me square in the stomach! I looked down and there it was, flat as a quarter, plastered to the front of my shirt! And, with no harm to me!

As time went on, I had a bullet part my hair and go through my hat and other times I was pelted by other bullets, but did no harm. None ever did draw blood. If I could only aim that kind of luck at the lottery. Just think!!!

RIVER LIFE

I may have mentioned elsewhere in this book that I grew up in a small town, Aurora, Indiana, along the Ohio River. My family's house stood on a hill overlooking the river just above the ferry landing.

I used to lie in bed of a morning and listen to the ferry blow its horn signals when it was going to leave shore and cross the river. When a towboat, pushing barges, passed by the signals would change so they would know which side to pass on, especially in the fog and there was always fog and steam rising off the water of a morning.

I had two cousins that worked on the ferry as deck hands. Sometimes in the afternoon I would strap on a pistol and go down to the ferry and ride back and forth across the river.

Whenever we were on the Kentucky side for any length of time, we would set up some cans on the bank and shoot them up. Occasionally my cousin Jim would bring his black powder cannon and we would shoot golf balls straight up in the air. For some strange reason they never came back down that we knew of. They must have hit somewhere inland.

My cousin Jim could not see well enough to get a driver's license, so he bought a boat. It was a fast boat too! He lived about a mile up North Hogan Creek and had his own dock. Hogan Creek fed into the Ohio River a couple hundred yards up river from the ferry landing. He could drive his boat to work if he wanted.

We were at one of the docks on the river gassing up one day when down the steps to the dock, came the town bully Mitchell M. and he was wanting us to take him skiing on the river. Jim and I looked at each other and said, "Sure hop in."

We went down the river a piece where there was no boat traffic and put Mitchell in a life jacket and threw out the tow line. I asked him if he really knew how to ski and he said oh yes. I was doubtful to say the least, but we put him in the water and handed him the skis. Mitchell got all ready and yelled, "GO!"

Away we went and Mitchell got up on the skis his first try! He seemed a little shaky at first but then smoothed out and was doing well. I told Jim to pour on the speed and let's see what the boat will do. We were zooming down the river now at break neck speed and I told Jim it is time to make a U turn and go back up river, but don't slow down on the turn.

Jim turned the boat and Mitchell came whipping around like a bullet. As he swung around he couldn't hang on

Life as I Lived It

and off he flew! I had never seen a human body skip like a rock off the water like that. He must have skipped five or six times before he splashed in the water to stay. It was hilarious. Well, to us anyway. We went back and scooped him up and took him back to the dock. I think that was the last time he went skiing, at least with us! He was done.

I don't live near the river anymore, but I visit it often. I miss the sounds and the smells.

SHARP KNIFE

Do you know how to sharpen a knife? Have you ever sharpened or tried to sharpen one?

When I was in high school, my shop teacher, Mr. Shelby, showed me how, using a real small sharpening stone by rubbing it in a circular motion on the blade That was okay, but it wasn't as sharp as it could be. It was only okay.

I was passing a friend of mines house one day and I noticed he was cleaning some snapping turtles in his shaded driveway. So, I stopped and parked and went to watch.

My friends name was Dutch B. and he had a meat market where he was the butcher. He had done it for many years and as he worked on the turtles, I couldn't help but notice how sharp his knives were. I asked him how he gets his knives so sharp and that I can't seem to sharpen mine very well no matter how hard I try.

Dutch said to stop by the store and he would show me how to sharpen a knife. So, I did, the very next day.

Life as I Lived It

We went behind the meat counter and he got out a nice sized sharpening stone, which was fine on one side and rough on the other.

He put oil on the fine side and showed me how the oil would roll in front of the blade when you had the knife blade at the correct angle while pushing the knife along the stone.

Then to make it even sharper, you use a butcher's steel, which is like a giant ice pick with fine flutes up and down it, to fine hone the edge like a razor blade.

I said. "Where do you get a stone like that?" Dutch said, "Down the street at the hardware store." So, I went there and bought a stone exactly like his. This was good.

Later on in years, I bought a professional three stone set-up that will revolve in an oil bath, which I usually keep hidden away for its own safe keeping.

We had just finished skinning a deer one day, when my Nephew, Jim, said his knife was getting pretty dull and wanted to know if I had a sharpening stone he could use.

I told him sure; I have one on the table over there, just take the top off of it.

"Wow," Jim said, "I didn't know you had a professional stone set-up." Jim is a machinist and his favorite phrase is, "We're making memories", every time we do something new or different.

Richard W. Block

Jim once told me that I do more for him then his brothers have ever done for him.

I suppose it's true. I have taken him a lot of places and taught him a lot of things and I could write a book about him, but I don't have that much paper!

SINK OR SWIM

I don't think I would have ever learned to swim if it hadn't been for the Boy Scouts of America and the fact that you had to swim to become an Eagle Scout.

My cousin Bill was an Eagle Scout and my mother was always bringing it up to me, that if he could make the rank, so could I.

It did make me try harder, but I had this fear of water because I drowned when I was a youngster.

I was sitting in an inner tube, floating along in the creek, on one of our family outings, when my cousin Eddie, who was my age and part fish, came up from underneath and flipped me over, sending me to the bottom.

I can still see the muddy creek bottom and the bubbles rising as I lay there on my stomach among the rocks and mud, when all of a sudden I felt a hand grab me under my arm pit and lift me up and out of the water. It was Dick, Eddie's father, and he took me to shore, where a half gallon of water was forced from my lungs. Well, it seemed like a half gallon, anyway.

Richard W. Block

After all the coughing and hacking and regaining my senses, I stayed away from water because I was afraid of it and my cousin, almost ending my short life.

Buck C., my scoutmaster, tried time after time to get me into the water and teach me how to swim, but I always stayed in the shallow areas or on the sideline away from the water. During a scout swim night at the local swimming pool, Buck showed me how to float and that the human body can't sink as long as you have air in your lungs.

He was right. With a big breath of air, I discovered I would float each time and not sink to the bottom like I once did.

I think that was the straw that broke the camel's back. After that, I wasn't as terrified of water, as before. Heck, I could always float, if nothing else.

So, I came to the conclusion that swimming can't be that difficult, even for an extremely skinny kid like me. All I needed to do, is watch different people swim, to see how they do it and then do it myself.

I first learned to dog paddle, because I didn't like my head in the water, then came the breast stroke that I always do now.

As time passed, I learned all the other strokes and passed my swimming tests to get my ranks.

Nowadays, I can just about sleep in the water while I am floating. I love the water and have no fear of it, but I still don't like to dive off diving boards or pool sides.

Life as I Lived It

A dozen years ago I got into snorkeling. There is a whole new world in the ocean and I love to look at it every time I can in the Bahamas. Floating in salt water is far more easy than in fresh water. I could snorkel all day if the sun wouldn't fry my backside!

I know my limitations on how far I can dive down to pick things up from the ocean floor and make it safely back to the surface before I need a breath of air.

I have collected beautiful sea shells from all over the world and I give snorkeling lessons to Boy Scouts and other people who need pointers to make their snorkeling more enjoyable and easier.

A few years ago, a dry snorkel appeared on the market. I bought one and have used it ever since. It is virtually impossible to get sea water in your mouth when you use the dry snorkel. It has a special valve that closes the top of your snorkel tube if water tries to enter.

There is an adapter valve only, that is available, that fits in the top of open snorkel tubes, making them dry snorkels as well and it is far cheaper than buying a dry snorkel model complete.

I have had a moustache for over 30 years and I have never had a face mask that didn't leak. I did however, buy a diver's mask that has a purge valve built in and I can ballast water from inside my mask with little effort.

Richard W. Block

I saw films where even babies have the ability to swim at birth. It is a natural instinct.

When I see those things, I feel stupid, knowing that I already knew how to swim by instinct but my intelligence kept me from it!

SKIL

I walked into the electric supply house one day to pick up a few needed materials and there was a salesman demonstrating the latest thing in battery operated drills.

I was skeptical at first, to say the least. because my partner had a rechargeable battery drill and it seemed to always run out of pep about the time you needed it most, especially when you were in the middle of something. You then had to take time out and plug a charger into it for an overnight charging period before it was usable again. It never seemed to last too long anyway.

As the salesman demonstrated what the new drill could do, I noticed it had a removable battery pack that could be charged separately. Now that was something new, a real breakthrough, I thought. All you need is a spare battery or two, that are already charged and you are back in business! "How long does a battery last?" I asked. "Two hundred drilled holes or drive two hundred screws", was his reply. "And just how long does it take to charge one of those batteries?" I asked. "One hour quick charge will fully charge it and then it goes into a trickle charge mode if you leave the battery in the drop-in charger".

Richard W. Block

It was an amazing drill. It had a two speed transmission. One speed was high for drilling holes and the other low speed was for torque that gave the power to drive screws.

It was the Boar Gun by Skil. It was 12 volt and would twist the head off of a screw with little effort, unless you let off the trigger in time.

Most other battery drills were only 9 volt or less and you had to charge the whole drill overnight.

Wow! What a breakthrough I thought. This is what I have been waiting for, for a long time!

I took the drill from the salesman's hands and said "I'll take it!"

As I headed for the sales counter to pick up my other supplies, the salesman shouted, "Now wait a minute. You can't take that, it is my demo drill."

How much is it? I asked.

"I don't know, it is not on the market yet", he said, as he handed me the charger that went with it.

"Put it on my bill and get me a second one with extra batteries as soon as you can and call me when they are here," I said.

"Well, I guess I am done for the day, if you are taking the drill", said the salesman. He had probably been there all day anyway, so I figured he was probably glad to quit early.

Life as I Lived It

I had noticed in his brochures that they also offered a holster that fit the drill that you could wear on a belt, so I ordered two holsters to go with the two drills.

Everything arrived at the electrical supply house just in time for my next installation job at the new McDonalds restaurant under construction.

I always did a lot of the finish work along with the other trade workers before the McDonalds could open.

Well, the reception I got from everyone on the job was a loud rude one. I walked in with holstered drills on both hips. "Look! Its Wild Bill! Its two gun Pete! It's Annie Oakley!" I heard it all multiple times everywhere I went on the job site. They were "rolling in the isles", so to say and at my expense.

I thought to myself, "Laugh all you want boys, there is a new sheriff in town and you have no idea what is about to happen".

I had put the left boar gun on high speed with a drill bit in it and the right boar gun was set on low torque speed with a screw bit in it. Once those guns cleared their holsters and I put them to work, their laughter stopped and their jaws dropped.

I had drilled a hole with the left and drove a screw with the right like a one-two punch. I was going two to three times faster than everyone else.

Then the questions started pouring in. "How long will the batteries last?" I asked.

"Two hundred holes or two hundred screws each and the power packs recharge in only one hour, but that doesn't mean anything, because I have extra power packs. That means no down time! All I have to do is slap a fresh power pack in place and drop the weak one into the quick charger". I told them.

A short time later, I walked onto the next new McDonalds job site, to do my part and I see a Boar gun power pack in its charger. It wasn't mine. I always engrave my name on all my tools. It is surprising how many tools come back home to roost when your name is on it.

As I looked around, I noticed several Skil Boar guns in use.

I think it was my turn to laugh!!

SNAKES IN THE ATTIC

I bought my farm from a bank in Milan, Indiana. Milan is the little town that won the State Basketball Championship in 1954. Milan is the actual town they made the movie Hoosiers about.

The farm property was in a very run down condition, with no useable buildings on it. A logger had owned the place and cut every tree that was worth anything and sold them. When he finished bleeding the place dry, he dropped it in the banks lap, a foreclosure. I came along looking for a bargain and they nailed me.

I had a mountain of work to do, just to get the property useable for farming. One of the major tasks was the renovation of the one story concrete block house. It was trashed to say the least.

I came up with a blueprint of my own design that would add a second floor and change the look of the whole house. Above the second floor, there was an attic crawl space with lights for storage. It was accessed through a panel door in the closet ceiling in one of the bedrooms.

Richard W. Block

One day we opened the panel door to store some things. My son Mike was on a step ladder and he grabbed the string to pull on the attic light, only, it wasn't the string he thought it was and it pulled out of his hand and took off to someplace else! It was the tail end of a 5 foot long black snake! That was the first time we discovered there were snakes living in my attic.

I can't say that I like snakes, but I will tolerate them as long as they stay out of sight and don't invade my living space.

Now that I was aware of my house guests, I kept an eye out for them and I discovered that they came out in the summer to feed on the mice in and around the buildings and then stayed in the attic crawl spaces in the winter. I used to hear the mice running around in the ceiling at night, but after a while the snake would catch them all.

I was never really sure how many black snakes lived up there but I was soon to find out.

One night we had a rain storm, followed by high winds. My son Robbie was at home and I was out of town. He called me on the phone and informed me that a huge oak tree had fallen on the house and crushed my bedroom to the floor and rain was pouring in, what should he do about it? "Nothing", I said. I told him I will take care of it tomorrow when it is daylight and I can see the damage. I was lucky I had not been in bed. The tree limbs were like a pitch fork through my bed!

I called Jake, an Amish builder, with whom I was acquainted. He came out with a huge tarp that covered most of the house. That kept the weather out for the present until he could get back to make repairs on the house.

Once the repair work started, I told Jake that I had a 5 or 6 foot black snake living in the attic, that was now open, and to leave it alone if he or his crew should happen upon it.

As you know the Amish don't drive, so they hire a driver with a van to take them to their job site every day. The driver works too, he doesn't just provide transportation.

Close to the jobs end they lost their driver and had to hire another. About his second day on the job, they were building some concrete forms, when the new driver came running up with a 5 foot black snake in his hand all excited yelling look what I killed with my hammer!

Jake about had a heart attack! He forgot to tell the new guy about the snake. Jake told me later that he told the new guy to get rid of the snake in the woods so I wouldn't find out about it.

The only reason Jake told me about it was because he discovered that there were more than just that one. A couple of days later, a 5 footer crawled upon the porch and laid there for a while, watching the guy's work, before going on his way.

I still don't like snakes, but I still tolerate them. They are welcome because they do a good job controlling the rodents.

SOME PEOPLE

I spent 25 years working at McDonalds as a Manager and Supervisor. In that length of time, I could say, I've seen just about everything imaginable.

Like the time our security cop caught the kid taking a leak on the back of the building and made him mop it up and the wring the mop out by hand.

Then the time the cop chased a kid through the lobby, spraying mace at him. He didn't catch the kid, but he sure got rid of all the customers!

Then there was the kid who came to the counter to order his fourth Big Mac. He was showing off for some of his buddies and was real proud of himself for eating three and was going for the fourth! I told him the fifth one would be fee but he had to eat it here for everyone to see! And he did!!! I bet he trashed his bathroom later on!

There were just a few events at one McDonalds where I was manager.

Life as I Lived It

Trashing a bathroom reminds me of another McDonalds across town where I was a maintenance supervisor at a later date. My job was to take care of any problems, any of our 42 stores had. A great deal of the repairs I did myself. I saved my employer thousands of dollars each year, which more than justified my position and salary.

I don't know why people like to destroy restrooms, but they just do. In this particular instance, this guy would go into the men's restroom and punch a hole in the wall with his fist, right through tile, drywall and all. I don't know if he was mad at someone or just trying to be macho.

Most of the time it's a onetime thing, but this guy would come back after repairs and do it again. After the second time, I decided there would not be a third. Instead of replacing the drywall and putting the tile back like normal, I reinforced the wall interior with a 2x4 studding with plywood instead of drywall, and the put the tile back. No difference could be detected, because it was all inside the wall. It figured it would take a bulldozer to do any harm this time.

A few days later the manager informed me that a young man with four broken fingers and a broken wrist was removed from the restroom by his buddies. No one seemed to know what had happened because there was no damage to be found in the restroom. But then, that's life. Some people just have to learn the hard way.

SPIDER BITE

One spring day I got this bite on my left leg up high near my crotch. I thought it was just a chigger bite because it itched and looked like one.

I had been picking raspberries along the railroad tracks and I hadn't tied my pant cuffs down or put on some bug spray.

The bite didn't seem to want to heal. I would put antiseptic on it of a morning but it would be raw at night. I thought maybe my clothing was rubbing on it and not letting it heal.

I was beginning to get pretty concerned about it because I was getting ready to leave town for a convention in Chicago. I was going to take a bus load of McDonald Managers and supervisors to the convention.

My wife said I should go to the ER at the hospital and get the bite looked at. So, I took my eight year old son with me on the pretense that they might take care of me quicker if I had a child with me.

Life as I Lived It

They had me strip and put on a gown and sit on a gurney in a private room. Doctors would come in from time to time and look at the bite, say nothing and then leave. Finally, a doctor returned with a swab. He said, "Do you see how the bite is shaped like a volcano?" Then he would poke at the bite with the swab and say, "see how when I poke it, a drop of blood appears on top?" "That is a spider bite. Do you see the red streak running down the inside of your leg to your ankle?" I said, "That's the first time I've noticed that, it wasn't there this morning!"

The Doctor then told me that my white cell count was about down to zero and that my body was losing the battle and that I was dying if I let it go. I needed to be put on an I.V. right away. I said, "Fine, let's do it now".

The nurse brought in the I.V. on a stand and began putting the needle in the top of my hand. She tried once, twice, three, four and five times but she couldn't seem to hit the vein and get it to flow. Finally she got it in the right place and as she started the flow, I felt this warming glow sensation coming over me and I said to her that I had better lay down.

The next thing I remember is the smell of ammonia and opening my eyes to see a bunch of doctors and nurses feeling me up and down all over. I said, "what the heck is going on?" One of the doctors told me that I had passed out and crashed onto a tray of tools before hitting the floor like a bag of wet cement. They were checking me for broken bones. I said that I was okay. The nurse said that the needle prodding must have affected me, but I told her no, it was the effect of the I.V. Entering my body.

Richard W. Block

I don't know what kind of little spider bit me, but the doctor said that if I had gone to Chicago, I would not have come back!

All of that, from a tiny little spider bite. I can only hope the spider died an agonizing death from biting me!!!

THE 4 HANDGUN HUNTING RULES

I HAVE FOUR RULES I GO BY WHEN I HUNT WITH A HANDGUN AND THESE RULES ARE AS FOLLOWS:

1. You have to be in range.
2. You have to have a rest.
3. You have to hit your target with your first shot.
4. You have to be the coolest cookie in the woods.

When people ask me how I can hunt with a handgun and get anything, I tell them these rules, and when they look puzzled at me because they don't understand, I explain in detail.

No 1. You have to be in range. What's in range? In range has no given footage or measurement. In range is different for each shooter. In range is the distance at which you feel comfortable that you can hit your target and that can vary at times, depending on whether your target is sitting, standing, laying or moving around.

No. 2. You have to have a rest. You have to rest your handgun on a solid object for support. If there is nothing available, go into the sitting position, using your knee for support. Because the distance from your front sight to your rear sight is very short, the slightest movement can cause the largest miss, so you have to realize that maintaining a steady sight alignment is crucial.

No. 3. You have to hit your target with your first shot. If you miss, the target will surely run. Any shots at this point are just throwing lead. This creates frustration on the shooters part and it also educates the target that you are a threat to be avoided in the future!

If you're first shot misses, just sit still and watch your target's reaction. It may not run or it may only run a short distance, in which case, you may get another chance to shoot again. If the target runs away, let it go and let it wonder what it was that caused it to run. If it doesn't know, then it won't be so wary of you when you next meet.

No. 4. You have to be the coolest cookie in the woods. What I am saying here is that you have to be composed, dead calm, determined and dedicated to making a kill. Totally focused, with no second thoughts. You must decide where you want the bullet to hit before you pull the trigger.

When you shoot at a paper target, you are aiming to hit the black bulls eye not the big white piece of paper. If you are not happy with the scores on your paper target, then get another handgun that will get the results you require!

Remember, aim small, miss small.

Never use handgun targets. Hell, anybody can hit a target the size of a barn! Get 50 foot rifle targets and place them

Life as I Lived It

60 yards out and shoot those with your handgun... That is what I do.

One of two things will happen when you have hunted with a handgun. If you did everything right, you will be pleased with yourself and the results of the hunt and want to go again.

If you messed up on one of the rules, you may return home so mad and disgusted, that you will be swearing to never hunt with that darn handgun ever again!!

THE AMAZING GLUE

I was visiting an old Scoutmaster friend by the name of Bob who had a farm near me in Moores Hill where I hunted on occasion.

Bob had just cut his thumb on the low thick part by his palm with a butcher knife before I arrived. I looked at it and could see it would easily need about five stitches to close it. I told him he had better get that taken care of right away as I left.

I saw him a week later and asked him how many stitches he had gotten. He said, "None" and showed me his cut. It looked to be about two weeks along in healing! I exclaimed, "That's impossible", because I knew that cut was only a week old and a bad one at that!

Just from my own experiences, I knew for a fact that it takes an average of about thirty days for a cut to heal. I've often remarked that if I had a dollar for every stitch my doctor had put in me, I'd be rich! I kept the doctor very busy when I was growing up. Believe me!

Life as I Lived It

I said to Bob, "How can this be? There are no stitches either! What happened after I left last week? Did you go to the doctor?" He said, "No I used Krazy Glue". I said, "You have got to be kidding!"

Then he explained that he had been reading an article in a medical journal about the use of a glue to repair intestines during surgery instead of using stitches which cause problems and have to be removed at a later date. Plus they scar the tissue and still cause problems even after removal.

The glue was in use in Europe and Canada, but not in the U.S.A. yet, so it had been marketed as Krazy Glue and Super Glue with a little change to the formula, but still almost the same.

That's why the direction of use, caution you not to get it on your skin, because that's what it's for, to glue skin!

"But, how did you get the cut closed", I asked, because it was a wide open cut. Bob said, "I just started at one end with a drop of glue and held it together for a few seconds until it held and then another drop here and there until I worked my way to the other end closing it up as I went". I could use my hand immediately as if it was never injured. "As you can see, it has advanced the healing process considerably", he said.

I got some Super Glue and kept it with my tools at work because I was always getting cut on my hands, especially on my knuckles when I was doing repairs on the job. This was always an aggravation to me because I needed all

Richard W. Block

my fingers to get certain tasks done in good time and fumbling along with an injury was very time consuming.

It was amazing. Every time I would cut a knuckle I would put a drop of Super Glue on it and put it back together! I found I could instantly use my finger as if no cut had occurred! No matter how much I flexed it!

I was at one of my neighbors one evening, I had just walked in to find one of the other neighbors who was there had cut himself and they were debating whether to get him stitched up. It didn't look so serious that a little Super Glue couldn't handle, so I whipped out my glue and all was well, but I warned him that on the third day to re-glue the spots where I had glued because it will let go without a follow-up gluing. That's the way it had always worked for me.

They were all shocked at my actions until I told them Bob's story. They became instant believers.

A couple of months later, the same neighbor I had used the glue on, left a phone message on my answering machine calling for help and to bring my glue.

I went to his home to find him passed out in a pool of blood on his sofa. He had cut off his ear in a scuffle with someone else and needed help.

I glued his ear back on and left him a note that I had been there and in three days he would need a few more drops to reinforce the ones in place now. His ear healed completely and he became a celebrity in all the bars with his glued on ear. He got a lot of free drinks for a good long time showing it off.

I am not saying for everyone to go right out and get Super Glue and use it on their selves, because it can cause a serious infection if used wrong.

THE BAND-AID

The Boy Scout Troop was touring Monticello, Thomas Jefferson's home, when I noticed several of the boys were gathered together debating something.

I went over to see what was going on. One of the boys had a large band aid on his leg and wanted to take it off, but he didn't want to fore go the pain of his leg hairs being pulled as the band aid was pulled loose.

I said to him, "I can pull that band aid off and you won't feel it at all." He was skeptical to say the least. "That's Impossible," he said. I said, "Its possible okay and I can take that band aid off and you won't even know it's gone!"

He then said, "Okay, let's see you do it". He then said, "I know what you're going to do. You're going to rip it off quick!" I said, "No. If I did that, you would feel it, wouldn't you?" He said, "Yes", of course.

By this time, everyone was watching to see how I was going to make the band aid disappear painlessly. I asked him, as I held on to the end of the band aid, "Do you know anything about horses?" He said, "No."

Life as I Lived It

I said, "Well, a horse is an animal with a one track mind. A vet can take a stick like tool with a piece of small chain attached to it, which is called a twitch and grab hold of a horses upper lip with it, and be able to do anything he wants to the horse, because the horse is concentrating on his upper lip!"

"Now you take a human being for example." There's a muscle right here on top of your shoulder, beside your neck, (I reached up and touched his shoulder as I talked), that is very sensitive."

At that moment, I squeezed the muscle between my thumb and forefinger causing him a sharp pain and also at the same time, I pulled the band aid off.

I let go of the muscle in the next instant and said, "That's a real sensitive muscle, isn't it?" He said, "Yes, it sure is!" Then I said, "Okay, Now, where is the band aid?"

He looked down and the band aid was gone! Everyone else looked too. It had disappeared! I said, "Here ya go," and I put the band aid in his hand, to his amazement.

"You have a lot in common with a horse," I told him as we moved on with the rest of the tour.

THE BANK

Do you ever think about your bank?

You go there and borrow money or to pay money back, but why is it called a Bank?

How did it get the name? Who named it that? How did someone determine it should be called by that name?

Well, I will tell you to the best of my ability. It all started long ago in Germany.

It was not proper for a German businessman to lend or borrow money, so they had to find a way to keep from going out of business in a time of need.

So, now enters the Jewish businessman. The Jewish businessmen had no problem of lending money and making money. They rarely had to borrow because they controlled most of the money in German communities.

On Sunday mornings they would set up a bench outside the churches and do their lending to the prominent businessmen as they came from church. The German word for bench is Banc.

As they immigrated to American, the practice came with them. Typical of American to spell things like they sound, Banc became Bank.

Makes a little sense now, doesn't it!

THE BRUSH PILE

You know, I don't remember when I first met Wilford S., it seems like I always knew him most of my life. He was a retired railroader and a craftsman with his own shop next door to the National Muzzle Loading Rifle Association in Friendship, Indiana. Wilford was a gunsmith and a well-known name in the muzzle loading community.

I was just a kid out of high school in the mid 1960's when I frequented his shop. Sometimes I'd drop off and pick up guns from different sport shops, so I got to know this pipe smoking, storytelling, backwoods advice giving, Kentucky Colonel (whose document of appointment by the Governor of Kentucky hung on his shop wall) pretty well.

I'd stop for a 5 minute pick up and be late for work 4 hours later. You just hate to break off a good conversation especially when he was talking about his younger years and working on guns for people such as Johnny Dillinger, who was an Indiana boy from a few miles away.

My Grandpa left behind a Winchester 12 gauge double barrel shotgun which I rarely used, but when I did, there

Life as I Lived It

was always something internally broken in it, which caused different problems each time Wilford repaired it.

As I was picking up Grandpa's relic shotgun one day after about the fifth or sixth repair, Wilford gave me this piece of his wisdom and advice. He said, and I quote, "You know, they haven't made parts for that gun for years and none are available. I've hand made about every part in it so far. My advice to you is to find a farmer who is clearing land and has made a huge brush pile, trade him your gun for the brush pile. Some cold winter day, burn that brush pile and get warm by it. You will be dollars ahead!!"

I passed Grandpa's shotgun along to another family member shortly thereafter. However, there are times when I've had cars that I'd like to trade for that darn brush pile!!!

THE BUGLE

In the mid 1970's, I worked for a restaurant chain which encompassed the greater Cincinnati area with its 42 stores. I normally spent my workday traveling from store to store repairing anything that needed it or solving whatever problems that arose. I would pass all types of homes, schools, businesses, shops etc. you name it, and I saw it.

Occasionally, something would catch my interest enough to entice me to stop and check it out, for instance, this small antique shop on the eastside that I frequently passed. I walked in and looked around at the assortment of items commonly found in such a shop. I deemed it average and was about to leave when I saw this civil war era bugle hanging by a nail on one of the roof beams.

It was in very good condition, over a hundred years of tarnish and very few dents! "How much is it?" I asked. "Thirty five dollars" was the reply. A more than fair price, but what would I do with it other than hang it on the wall? I did not play a bugle.

I told my wife about it that evening and I was debating whether to buy it or not.

Life as I Lived It

I returned the following morning but the shop was not opened yet. I peered through the window and could see the bugle hanging on the rafter. I had work to do close by, so I'll just stop by after the shop opens and buy it, I thought.

I returned only a couple of hours later to discover the bugle had been sold only moments earlier and was gone! I could not believe I let it slip through my fingers.

Oh well, such is life.

Many months passed and I was unwrapping my Christmas present from my wife in an old shoe box of mine. I lifted the lid and guess what, there's that darn bugle again! Except with one big difference, she polished it! Over a hundred years of tarnished history erased! It looked brand new! Oh no! I couldn't believe it!

I was really surprised, but more surprised to see it wasn't a plain brass bugle but a brass and copper bugle with a silver mouth piece and chain! I still miss the hundred plus years of tarnish though.

THE BUMPER

Have you ever had parts left over after repairing something, like a car for instance?

Well, in this case it was nothing serious or overlooked, it was just an extra part that I already had and I didn't have any use for it. It was a bumper that fit my 1953 Chevy.

I don't remember why I had an extra bumper but there it was and I needed to get rid of it.

One evening, my close friend Bill P. and I were out looking for some sort of mischief to get into, as usual, when we decided that the time was right to get rid of the bumper.

I told Bill that I had heard from a good source that the telephone company had dumped a bunch of their old telephones in the creek below town, for lack of any better idea of what to do with them and that seemed to be a good place to deposit the old bumper. What the heck, we'll just add to the underwater pile!

Life as I Lived It

"Sounds good to me", was Bill's reply. So we loaded the old bumper in the back of my pick-up truck and headed for the creek.

Now, in case you are not familiar with what a bumper off a 53 Chevy is like, it's a big bulky heavy bumper, unlike the bumpers of this day and age. It takes two people to handle it, just moving it around!

We stopped in the middle of the bridge above the creek that fed into the river. It was a deep creek and lots of people fished there in the evenings after dark. They would sit on the bank beside their lanterns until late at night on weekdays and sometimes all night on weekends.

Well, this night was no exception. The creek banks were dotted with several lanterns in the dark as we looked over the side of the bridge just to see if anyone was there.

Suddenly a thought struck me. I looked at Bill and said "ya wanna have some fun?" Bill's reply as always was, "absolutely!"

"Let's do one of our fight routines, like we are beating the holy hell out of someone and then we'll throw the bumper over the side!" was my reply.

It was all we could do to keep from laughing while we were trying to act serious!

We started out arguing in gruff voices and then the fight began, smacking our fists in our hands and throwing ourselves about, bouncing and thumping against the side of the truck in the dark of the night.

After the scuffle had gotten everyone's attention, with a few loud, "take that and that, you S.O.B," we grabbed the bumper by each end and over the side it went.

After the big splash, the rather loud remark, "guess he won't mess with my girl anymore!" was announced, as we jumped into the truck and sped away.

What wasn't heard, was the profuse laughter going on in the truck, as we sped on down the road and out of sight in the darkness. We were busy laughing at the shocked look the people down on the creek bank had on their faces and betting whether the creek would be dragged for a body tomorrow.

Heck, some of them were already running for their cars, before we even reached the end of the bridge!

aaahhh…..such is life in a small rural town!

THE CEMENT MIXER

Living on a hillside in an old three story house, is what prompted me to learn all about cement and how to use it in all kinds of applications. It was actually more of a necessity than a desire.

Our old house on Market Street was built in 1810 before Indiana was even a state. The rear wall and both end walls of the first floor were laid stone, set back into the hillside with the front and two upper stories being frame in structure of mostly poplar. Poplar wood was a common building material in those days because it was straight, strong and plentiful.

It's truly amazing how long those laid stone walls have lasted and held their shape with no real mortar to hold them together! Laying stone like that was a real art in those days.

We had tall laid stone walls in front of the house down on the street level, as well as what used to be an old carriage house, which was also set back into the hillside.

Richard W. Block

I remember, when I was very small, my dad tearing down the front of the carriage house and the roof coming down with it, as it collapsed in a pile among the three stone walls that made up the rest of the structure. We used to call it, "the garage hole."

I used to keep a pile of sand in there, along with a utility trailer with gravel in it for making cement.

We had walls on each side of the house which separated our property from the neighboring properties.

Everything moves around on a hillside. Nothing stands still or stays in place, especially when seasons change.

My neighbor, Austin B. "Baldy" as he was known, lived downhill from us and was a retired "jack of all trades" person who taught me all about cement, carpentry and plumbing.

When a wall got to be in pretty bad shape, my mom would tear it down and then say to me, "It's your turn, put it back." These kinds of projects get real old, real quick, especially the second time around on the same wall!

Baldy suggested putting the wall back with cement mortar instead of just laying the stones in place like before. This way it's permanent if you do it right. He showed me how to lay stone and vent the walls so they wouldn't trap moisture and stay in place where they belonged. I carried a bucket of mixed cement mortar in each hand, up the steps from the garage hole down on the street, to each project site until the job was finished. That was a lot of back breaking work.

Life as I Lived It

Mixed cement is not light by any means, especially when you've just spent time and energy mixing it and then you've got to use it when you get it to where the work site is! I did all of this by myself and by hand of course.

One of my Dad's friends had a cement mixer. We were at his farm one day when I noticed it. I asked him if it worked and he said yes, all you have to do is plug it in and you're ready to go. I told him that I never used one before but I'd sure like to borrow it and give it a try. He showed me how to use it and so I did. That was the end of mixing cement by hand. I was hooked.

The only thing I didn't like about it was that it was so cumbersome to move around. It would be ideal if it only had wheels. I looked up mixers in the Sears catalog and guess what; they had the same mixer in a model with wheels on one end, so you could move it around easily. That was it! I bought it! But you know how Sears is, it came in a half dozen boxes and I also had to assemble it! The first thing I ever bought with wheels was a car, when I graduated high school and had a job in 1966. The second thing I bought with wheels was the cement mixer.

The car is long gone, but the cement mixer is family. It's here to stay; I've had that mixer for over 45 years now. I've used it everywhere. I've loaned it out and I've turned down many opportunities to sell it. Every time someone makes an offer, I say, "I'm sorry, but its family, and you just don't sell family." I'm sure most people don't understand that statement, but if we were talking about a dog or some living thing, they might understand then.

Baldy used to point out the seams or edges of the cement and the size of the gap between structures. He'd say, "Look at the gap when winter comes, concrete breathes, it expands and contracts according to what season it is. There's nothing you can do about it except plan for it when you build something." I've always remembered that bit of advice and used it to my every advantage over the years.

As time went on at the old house, the rear wall in the "garage hole" was getting in pretty bad shape. It was a laid stone wall about ten feet plus tall and it was falling apart about half way up with a huge hole beginning to show and the appearance of perhaps buckling and collapsing unless dealt with.

Baldy had shown me how to lay block, so I decided to build a block wall out in front of the old stone one, which is what I did.

To make sure it stayed; I put rebar down into the ground, through the centers of the holes in the concrete blocks and then filled them with mortar, making them solid, I filled all the concrete blocks with mortar as I built the wall layer after layer. When I left off for the day, I only filled the blocks half full, so when I continued, the next row would lock in place when I filled them all in mortar. As the wall grew taller, I would fill in between the two walls with concrete and steel, which including the thickness of the old stone wall, probably made the whole wall about three to four feet or more thick! After the wall was finished at the desired height, I built another wall of stone, on top but behind the new wall, to divert water away from the walls when it rained or snowed.

Life as I Lived It

Over forty years has passed and that wall stands as a monument still, with not even the slightest sign of a crack in it!

That's impossibility, but yet, there it is. I evidently did something extremely right to defy the forces of Mother Nature and win. It baffles me to this very day when I think about it.

I also developed an unusual way to pour a concrete floor in the old root cellar that has never cracked either. I used my left over mortar from other projects and just mad angular forms, according to how much left over mortar I had, which determined their size. I used no steel reinforcement in the concrete at all. The forms took the shape of trapezoids, triangles and parallelograms, which all locked into each other creating a floor which reinforced it by its own design. It was poured right on top of the old dirt floor with no subbase of pea gravel or anything.

When I think back about this time era and all those projects and how immense some of them were, I wonder how I ever found the time and energy to get them all accomplished. It's kind of like the story about the ant, moving the rubber tree plant. If you keep after it little by little, eventually the "high hopes" become reality.

I can still see old Baldy in my mind, signing one of my merit badge applications for the Boy Scouts when I was working on my Eagle rank.

I am probably the only person to ever earn the Masonry merit badge in our scout troop! After our Scoutmaster,

Richard W. Block

Buck C. passed away, the eagle scouts who had been in his troop met at the scout camp. We built a campfire ring in tribute to Buck, which would be named after him and be used by all scouts and their families, there at Camp Maumee, in the Hoosier National Forest. It was like a reunion. People I hadn't seen in years

Were there, working like an army of beaver. Which was the better tribute I wonder, the monumental ring, or the scouts who made it happen?

My cement mixer was there too. It was in charge of building the two huge altars on which the fires would be built for the weekly ceremonies at camp. They were concrete block, with Bedford stone facing on all four sides, with a fire brick top, to resist the heat of the fires which would burn on top of them in the future years to come.

Dave H. had a bronze plaque made about Buck and with the help of Nick U., Dave and Bob B.; we designed and built a monument of stone and geodes, overlooking the whole project.

With a lot of mortar and a bunch of brother eagles, "we moved that darn rubber tree plant!"

THE COLLECTION

Have you ever been a collector of anything? It's not hard to be a collector; all it takes is interest, a little time and the opportunity to be able to get what you want.

I used to carpool to meetings near Bloomington, Indiana with several others. That's what you do when you're on a committee, in any kind of volunteer organization, in your so-called spare time. The person who supplied the transportation was a rock collector, geodes, to be precise.

The Bloomington area is the geode capital of the mid-west. A geode is a round, softball sized, light brown stone that resembles a head of cauliflower. It is usually hollow with crystals inside if you cut or break it open.

He was much older than I and preferred someone else to drive his car so I usually drove. The roads turn to gravel as you near the meeting place and are graded periodically by the highway department, grader which, occasionally "turn up" geodes.

As I would pass one by, he'd say, "look! There's one!" I'd say, "Yep, it sure was". He'd say, "Aren't you going to stop?" I'd say, "Nope, you don't want that one."

After several times of this scenario, I stopped at the gateway to our meeting place where two pillars made of geodes and concrete stood. He asked, "Why are we stopping her?" I said, "Get out and I'll show you where the geodes grow." (As if they do!)

I took him into the woods and raked away the top layer of leaves, revealing hundreds of geodes as they lay on the ground. (That's where the unused geodes for the pillars were discarded years before!)

He was elated! He filled his car to the point of almost dragging the ground... He'd been collecting geodes for years and didn't have a tenth of what he had just loaded up!

I asked, "What will you do with all those geodes?" He replied, "The same thing I always do, except this time I'll finish the job of bordering my flower garden with them!"

THE COW HORN

When I was a youngster growing up in the 1950's rural scene, I like the rest of the American youth, watched T.V. every evening.

One of my favorite programs, besides the Westerns, was Leave it to Beaver.

Everybody used to watch that show. It is still shown on the cable network today.

Beaver's brother, Wally, had a friend call Lumpy Rutherford, who drove an old Ford convertible jalopy in some of the episodes. Occasionally, Lumpy would blow the horn on his car. He had a unique horn called a cattle caller. It mad the moo-in sound of a cow when blown. It was a hoot!

That horn was the funniest thing on the show and I vowed that one day, when I am old enough to have my own car, I would have one of those horns too!

As time came to pass, I had my own car and I hunted down a source to supply me that cattle calling horn, which

Richard W. Block

I found to be J.C. Whitney's in Chicago. I bought three of them over a period of time!

It was an amazing horn. It mounted under the hood with a cable and had a lever on the steering column to control it with. The farther you pushed the lever, the louder it bellowed just like a bull! Wow!!! I had the only one around.

It had such a distinctive sound that every time I blew it, everyone knew it was me coming down the street. I put one on my Mother's car too, and when she was in town, she would blow her cow horn and I would answer back with mine, letting her know I was in town too, so we could meet up.

I worked in downtown Aurora at the time and went to lunch at Frisch's restaurant between the towns of Aurora and Lawrenceburg, everyday at noon.

The route to lunch took me right by my old high school, which I had graduated from the previous spring of the year and was full of my friends and fellow schoolmates who were still in school.

As I passed by the school, I blew my cow horn, bellowing like an old bull, real loud and honoree. I noticed all the kids in the classrooms jumping up and running to the windows to see out and wave, as well as cheer me on. I thought to myself, "what a great pay-back to the school for all of those boring hours of classes".

Every day for an entire year, I made that horn bellow out loud as I passed by at noon and disrupted all the classes by doing so!!

Life as I Lived It

Aren't paybacks great??

After a while, the 12:00 noon siren at the firehouse became insignificant as the sound of the bellowing cow horn took its place. You could set your watch at school by the sound of the moo!!

I was at a 35 year class reunion recently. Can you guess the most talked about subject???

MOOOOOOO!!!!!!

THE CROSSING

One evening around 10:00 in the late fall, I was on my way home from a friend's house in the next county. It had been raining hard earlier in the week and the creeks were running high. Laughery Creek is the dividing line between Ohio and Dearborn Counties and empties into the Ohio River. I had traveled the long route to my friend's house which uses bridges over the creek because I knew it would be a safe route.

The tiny town of Hartford sits high on the bank overlooking Laughery Creek miles from the Ohio River. It has a normally dry ford which is a tremendous short cut to my home town of Aurora. A dry ford is a concrete roadway across a waterway with pipes beneath for the water to flow thru, thus the term "dry" ford.

I drove to the ford to check the water which I knew was flowing over the ford in great volume. I've known people and vehicles to be washed away here. I know this water well and it's power.

I judged the crossing to be border line safe. I could see where some trucks had crossed, but I was driving a

Life as I Lived It

compact car. I felt I could make it, so I drove carefully across with the water washing at me every foot of the way. I made it! It was too close for comfort. I opened my door and let the water out!

I drove on in the total darkness wondering why I wasn't swept away. I'd gone a mile and passed a man on foot. He looked soaking wet in the middle of nowhere. I stopped and offered a ride. He got in. I couldn't now see he was not only wet but hypothermia was setting in. I don't think he knew his own name. All he could mumble was "I lost my bike, (motorcycle) it's gone." He was not as lucky as I at the crossing. I finally discovered where he lived and delivered him home, sending him straight to a warm bath.

I guess his luck was me. Luckily crossing and finding him in the darkness. I never did know his name.

ENTERTAINER

I once knew a man who was an entertainer. He was a very talented musician that played a banjo, base fiddle and piano as well as a guitar, but he mainly was known for his banjo playing. He worked in night clubs most of the time and was the head of the Musicians Union in the Cincinnati area. His name was Ralph G. and he loved to spend his spare time on the Ohio River in his boat. He would invite guests and play his banjo and tell jokes while cruising up and down the river. He enjoyed good Canadian whiskey to the fullest extent and would spend all day fishing.

Fishing was his passion. He would rather fish than eat. My boss and friend Louis G. would invite Ralph up to his place in the top of Michigan for a week at a time and Ralph always came, fishing tackle and banjo in hand.

Louis and Ralph had been lifelong friends and were about the same age, both in their eighties at this time, but still able to get around pretty darn good.

Ralph would take a cooler and his fishing tackle onto Lou's pontoon boat and spend all day fishing on the fifty acre lake on Lou's ranch. Lou's ranch covered 800 acres with

Life as I Lived It

two lakes and multiple buildings with a few horses and buggies and miles of trails throughout the property.

There were lots of deer, elk, bear, wolves, coyotes and bald eagles, as well as all the small game animals too. It was always a trill to ride around in a golf cart and see what all you could find running around on the property!

I would tell Ralph to keep about a dozen of the largemouth bass and I would filet them for him and we would have a fish fry for everyone. I can still picture the delightful smile on Ralph's face when he put that first bite of fish in his mouth and close his eyes as if he was experiencing heaven.

I think I got him hooked on my batter recipe and cooking skills because he would invite me over to his home in Kentucky to fry up some bass filets that we would bring home from Michigan.

One day we noticed from the lake house that the pontoon boat with Ralph onboard had not moved around for a long period of time. We just thought the fishing must be good in that spot.

After a time, and the boat still had not moved I looked through the spotting scope in the lodge to see what he was doing. To my surprise, he was nowhere in sight and I could see the cover over the engine was propped up to reveal access to the motor. I thought I had better go see what is going on, so I jumped into a golf cart and headed to the other end of the lake where the boat was.

Richard W. Block

About half-way there I happened to spot the top of Ralph's head in the swamp by the water edge. I stopped and walked over to the edge of the trail, looking down at Ralph, who was resting on a downed tree at the water edge.

Upon hearing me arrive, Ralph said, "I am glad you are here, I don't think I could have made it back to the lodge." I told him I knew something was wrong when I could not see him on the boat. I helped him up the hill to the golf cart and the first thing he said was, "gee I did not know there was a road here! I have been going along the water edge through the brush, mud and downed trees trying to get back."

He was wearing shorts and his legs were cut and bleeding. He said the battery on the boat went dead and he could not get the motor started. I told him that I would take care of it and to go straight up to his room and take a shower and put on some long pants so Lou doesn't see his injuries. I told Ralph that if Lou finds out his mishap, he will stop letting him use the boat.

Meanwhile, I drove the golf cart over to the end of the lake where the pontoon boat had floated in to shore and I could get on board. Ralph did not tell me that he took the motor apart looking to find a manual pull start! But of course, there is none on that model motor. I had a fun time putting something back together that I didn't take apart!

After getting the motor back together, I discovered that the boat was in too shallow of water and the propeller was buried in the mud so it kept the motor from turning over fast enough to start and ran the battery down. I needed to get the boat back to the dock before Lou discovered it was

Life as I Lived It

not tied up in its proper place so I pulled the battery out and took it to the workshop for a quick charge. As soon as it was charged enough, I put it back and started the boat after I pushed it away from the shore and out of the mud. Back to the dock I went and tied off. Lou never knew any different.

I told Ralph to take one of the two-way radios with him next time. After all, a man in his late eighties doesn't need an ordeal of that magnitude at this time in his life.

Ralph served in the Army in World War II in the Music Corp because of his musical ability. They gave him a bugle and gave him a few days to learn how to play it. He told me he never did learn to play it because a week later a record of bugle calls showed up and all he had to do was play the phonograph. He did teach his Lieutenant how to play the piano however!

When Ralph died, he was cremated and they had a wake at the boat club on the Ohio River. There were many pictures of Ralph there and I made the comment that he has the same smile in each picture to his son Roddy. Roddy told me that Ralph was given lessons on how to smile for publicity photos.

After all was said and done they polluted the river with Ralph's ashes.

I think he would have gotten a big laugh out of that scenario! Especially if I had added that all the fish in that area of the ash dumping, were drunk for a week!

Ralph was a great guy and I miss him.

THE FLAG POLE

I HAVE ALWAYS BEEN VERY PATRIOTIC. If I had a dollar for every flag raising and lowering I have participated in, I would be a rich man today.

There is something majestic and captivating about watching those stars and stripes paint the breeze. I always admire one of those huge flags blowing in the wind that you see along the interstate highway as you travel by in your car.

Flags are so nice when they are clean and new, but they can be an embarrassment when they are faded and tattered. I see some really pitiful looking flags on display at times and I would really find joy in taking them down. I always wonder if their owners know how bad it makes them look to others when they are displaying a flag that should have been replaced long ago. Don't they care or don't they know any better, is what I always wonder.

There is a place of business not far from my home that I pass frequently. They have a really nice flag pole in front of their building. It is very tall with a large American flag flying on it. Every time I pass by I would like to stop and

Life as I Lived It

meet the person in charge and choke the living hell out of him for displaying the worst, most tattered U.S. flag I have ever seen in my life! It is so bad that the stripes are like independent streamers!

I remember the first flag pole I ever erected. It was in Michigan one November during hunting season at my boss's lodge along the Au Sable River. I took the ole double bit ax out of the tool shed and went in search for a suitable jack pine to make a flag pole out of, Paul Bunyan style. After I felled the chosen tree, I trimmed off all of the limbs and skinned off all of the bark, which produced a nice straight pole about 25 feet long and all accomplished with only that double bit ax, which was a familiar tool in my hands.

I dug a hole about three feet deep, striking water, with no surprise, using a posthole digger. After I secured a pulley and rope, I dropped the pole into place. It was like dropping it into a well! After tamping in the sandy dirt, I put a cleat on the pole to fasten the rope to when tying it off and snap clips to fasten to the flag. It looked great even without a flag on it! It was a nice addition to the lodge. Every time someone stayed at the lodge, the first order of the day was to put the flag up.

That pole served us well for many years, but then the inevitable happened, it rotted off at the bottom and fell over. But, wait! The caretaker planted two short posts on each side of the old pole, sticking about two feet out of the ground and placed the old flag pole in between with two long bolts passing through all three, making it better than originally!

Richard W. Block

Now you could remove one bolt and the other became a hinge that let the pole down for any needed repairs or painting! What a great improvement! Little did I know that this improvement would come into play in later years and in different places, the most recent being at my home in the city.

I had wanted to erect a flag pole in the yard ever since I did away with the post mount pole in the socket holder set-up. You know, the flag on a stick, set at an angle on people's houses. That is okay, but it doesn't serve the purpose of a pole.

Well, one day in the summer of 2004, opportunity knocked. I had a new garage built in the back yard and had eliminated a section of chain link fence. Among the left over materials was a twenty foot long top rail pipe which I immediately recognized as a good candidate for a flag pole, but where and how should I mount it?

After a long deliberation, I decided to put it next to my neighbor's bordering chain link fence near the street in front of our homes. I started digging the hole with the post hole digger, when I thought about how much shorter the pole will be if I plant it three feet in the ground. Then I thought of the Michigan flag pole and how the caretaker had saved it without losing a single inch of height, so I thought I will do it Michigan style!

So, to make a long story short, I sandwiched a piece of the pipe pole material between two pieces of pipe and concreted them in the ground.

Life as I Lived It

After the concrete dried, I removed the pipe spacer and replaced it with the pole that I had previously drilled and fitted with cap, rope and pulley. It hinged perfectly up into place on the bottom through bolt and stood straight as expected after putting the second through bolt in place.

Now it is just a matter of tying on the snap clips and installing the cleat to tie the rope off with. It matched the fence and it was a nice addition.

I had a nice 3x5 American Flag already, so I ran it up the pole as the finishing touch. It really looked nice and I received a lot of compliments on it.

As time went on, I discovered that the cheap printed flags worked a lot better than the more costly sewn nylon flags, being it took less of a breeze to float the printed cotton flag.

After the pole had been in place a couple of months, I discovered something about myself in relation to the flag on the pole. I had, without thought and very routinely, been using the flag to gauge the wind strength, direction and velocity, to determine the weather!

It would tell me how to dress when going out and from which direction to expect the weather to blow in from, as well as how fast it was going to get here.

It kind of makes you think about the many things one takes for granted, doesn't it?

THE FLAT TIRE

An event I will never forget is just about to happen.

The time is around 8:30 p.m., just a day or two before Christmas 1970. We were going to Logansport and then Valparaiso visiting relatives along the way.

It was cold and snowing a little as we proceeded up U.S. 31 above Indianapolis just south of Carmel when I heard that right rear tire blow and saw the hubcap pass me by disappearing into the white snow that blanketed everything. I was in the middle of nowhere, farm country, with only fields of snow. It had rained after the snow to make a layer of ice on top and it made a crunching sound as I drove my 1961 Chevy up onto a field entrance getting us just off the road, my wife and two small children holding their breath every inch. I had retrieved my hubcap when my wife informed me the spare tire was flat from a previous week and had kept it secret.

There I stood in the dark alongside the road, with spare tire and flashlight looking for a ride. There was no traffic, the weather was too bad. Then a lone driver came in his mustang. He passed me by, turned around and came back.

Life as I Lived It

Throw your tire in my back seat and get in was his reply. "I'm from Carmel and the last service station was closing as I left. We must hurry" he said.

We made it just in time and my tire only needed inflating. The driver took me back, where I discovered my wife had left the jack somewhere. He loaned me his. I changed the tire and as I returned his jack he said, "See if you can pull back onto the road and I'll watch." When I did, he left. I didn't even get to thank him. I've returned his good deed many times over the years to others in need of help and if he is reading this, THANKS.

THE HANDSHAKE

One day, my scoutmaster came up to me and stuck out his hand and said, "put her there!"

I was just a bewildered kid of about twelve years old and I, of course, took his hand and shook with him.

In the middle of the hand shaking procedure, he exclaimed out loud, "what is this? It feels like I have hold of a dead fish, all limp and clammy. Put a little grip to it. That's it. Don't be afraid to shake a man's hand."

Buck was a wise man and a good teacher.

I was taught how to properly shake hands.

I learned that how you shake a hand, projects an image of who you are.

People who grip to hard tend to be overbearing in nature and people who have a poor or weak grip, tend to be whimpy in nature, a real push over at times.

All these things can be projected in a simple, how do you do, handshake.

How do you measure up?

Think about it.

THE NAME GAME

I worked for McDonald's restaurants for 25 years. After working in store management for 3 years, I moved up into a supervisory position. I and another man, Mr. C. was in charge of all repairs, from the rooftop to the blacktop, in 42 McDonald restaurants in the Greater Cincinnati area.

As a result, we were in and out of multiple restaurants every day. We split up the market and we had 21 stores each. Each store had up to 80 employees each. Most of the people that worked at nights, you never knew at all, except for the managers, they rotated shifts weekly.

All of the crew people were required to wear a name tag, but the manager did not at that time, like they do now.

I bounced around from store to store and knew all the managers and the other supervisors by name.

The office staff top officers would occasionally make store visits, but were frequently at a loss for the names of some of the managers on the shift so they would seek me out and ask who were the managers working today and who was who.

Life as I Lived It

After being briefed, they would go and approach each manager, shaking their hand and greeting them by name.

The managers would always be impressed that the top management knew their names and greeted them as if they had known them all their lives and were their best of friends.

That was what got me into the practice of always looking at people's name tags because that is what they are for, so you don't look so stupid when you are working among other people and you need to know their names

I read Dale Carnige's book, "How to Win Friends and Influence People", where he states that there is no sweeter sound to a person's ears, than hearing his own name spoken.

It is true! Dale's book was required reading when I moved into the office staff and it is the only book I have ever read twice. If you haven't read it, you should. It will change your life a little and make you a better person for sure, especially when dealing with other people.

I had my name embroidered on my jackets and other clothing. When I was in supply houses picking up materials or parts, the people behind the counter would always call me by name, which would sometimes shock me, until I would realize they read my name on my jacket. So, I would do the same to everyone that had their name on display as well. A lot of people became my friends because of that.

Richard W. Block

It is fun to greet people you don't know in passing somewhere and call them by name and sometimes ask how they are, while at the same time, viewing this look of mystery on their face like where do I know this person from and it is all because of that silly little name tag.

I always make a point to learn what the waiter or waitress's name is, so I can use it in communicating with them. It helps to know your waiter's name if you need something and the service you get is usually much better because of the sweet sound of one's own name being heard in a room full of strangers.

THE NEPHEW

My newly acquired nephew, by marriage, Jim belongs to a gun club in Cincinnati. Belonging to a club in a big city, gives you access to a shooting range, where you normally have nowhere else to go to shoot.

He had heard that I liked to shoot, so he would invite me to go with him to the range to shoot occasionally, which I never seemed to have the time to go, but I appreciated the offer.

He was telling me one day that he would like to get a .357 magnum handgun and that he had never had anything larger than the .22 cal. Pistol he currently owned.

He was looking to me for help and advice, so I took him to a gun show that I go to occasionally and fixed him up with a good deal on a handgun that I knew he should do well with. He tried it out and elated over how accurate it was.

I told him to shoot some .38 specials in it at the range and he would be even more elated.

And he was!!! He did not know a .357 magnum could shoot three different cartridges, the others being cheaper and probably a little more accurate when shooting range targets.

He was telling me how much more accurate the .357 was compared to his .22 pistol.

I thought, something is wrong with this picture.

So I went to the range with him and I took one of my Browning Buckmark .22 pistols with me. I thought maybe I could give him a few pointers and at least give him some comparison between pistols.

I had never seen him shoot, but if he was happy with his large bore .357, he ought to do better with my pistol. He had a very popular brand pistol, but it was an older model with fixed sights. It was more of a collector's item than a shooter, even though it was like new. You couldn't hit anything with it. It threw bullets all over the target. I told him that if I ever needed a boat anchor, I would buy it from him!

I kind of expected it to be that way though. Even their newer models with adjustable sights don't do as well as they should. I'd shot many of them and they never impressed me, so I never desired to own one.

I slapped a loaded clip into my Browning and handed it to Jim. I said, "Here, try this. I think you'll get a whole new meaning of hitting a target." He shot the whole ten round clip, hitting everything he aimed at. He went ballistic.

Life as I Lived It

"Your pistol shoots like a rifle!" Jim exclaimed. I said, "Well compared to yours, it does!" "You need to get rid of your gun and get a better one." I told him. Jim said, "Can you sell mine for me at a gun show sometime? I said, "Sure, put a price on it." He did, and I sold it to a very happy collector.

I had seen a Browning Challenger III at a show for a fair price, so I took Jim there and advised him to buy it before someone else does. The Challenger III is a collector's item also.

I bought one when they first started to make them. You could say that it's the father of the Buckmark. They only made a few and immediately stopped production and came out with the Buckmark series of pistols which were cheaper to make.

I think I've only ever seen three or four of them including mine. I told Jim if he wasn't happy with the Challenger III, I'd buy it from him for the same price he paid for it and he wouldn't be losing a penny. It was still in its original box and was in like brand new condition. What a find!!

We took it to the range and loaded up. Jim starting shooting soda pop cans on the twenty five yard range. They call this the plinking range and people sit cans and clay pigeons out for targets against the hard dirt mound that serves as a backstop for the bullets.

I said, "What are you doing" Jim said, "I'm shooting cans." I said, "Stop doing that! You're embarrassing yourself and your pistol!" He looked over at me and I pointed down range at the dirt mound all cluttered with all kinds of debris. I said, "Do you see those little pieces of orange clay pigeons laying all over the backstop?" Jim said, "Yes". I said, "Pick out a chip about the size of a dime and shoot that. Hell anybody can hit those barn sized cans. Choose a target that is worthy of the weapon."

He shot the clips with ease and was instantly in love. "If I never own another pistol in my life, I'll be a happy man." Jim elated. "I never dreamed there could be a pistol as accurate as this." He said.

Just the other week, I invited Jim out to my farm to do a little shooting. We were heading down to the creek that borders my lower fields when I saw a squirrel run across the road and up a tree. I told Jim. "Let me introduce you to Nomad." Nomad was a cheaper version of the old original Challenger I model made back in the 1960's. Nomad is my favorite hunting pistol, with which I can shoot through the bullet holes of my other pistols with little effort.

Jim watched as I dropped the squirrel from the top of the tree with one shot, seen when I could only see a small portion of him as he hugged flat against the tree. He said he had never seen anything killed with a pistol.

I told him I was actually embarrassed to take such an easy shot. Later that day I let Jim shoot my Nomad. He was truly impressed. It was like petting a dinosaur, something that's wonderful and just as extinct.

THE OWL

I was squirrel hunting one day in August when I heard the crows. They were across a field in another section of the woods, a good distance away.

I had been in the woods only a short time. The long climb from the Hogan Creek Valley was a steep and tiring one. This was a first time hunt in this particular area and I was still figuring out the lay of the land. By that, I mean I was checking out the location of the nut bearing trees and if they had nuts on them and if the squirrels were eating them.

The area was plentiful in Hickory trees but few had any nuts at all and what few there were, were already cut up. By cut up, I am referring to how squirrels get to the actual meat of the nut, by cutting away the outer hull and nut shell with their teeth. The shavings that fall to the ground are called cuttings, which when plentiful, almost form a carpet on the ground, which tells how active the squirrels are in that tree.

Sometimes when there is not enough rain in the spring of the year, only a few trees will get enough rain water

Richard W. Block

to enable them to bear nuts. (It works the same with blackberries too.)

When this is the situation, the squirrels all feed on the only trees with the nuts on them, a common sense happening.

Sometimes you can get your limit of five squirrels out of one tree.

Well, it just so happens that in this area that I was hunting, there were few to no nuts, indicating to me that the squirrels had probably moved on to greener pastures, so to speak.

It was hard to hear anything because the crows were making such a racket.

So I thought to myself, since the squirrel hunting looks pretty poor, I thing I'll just slip on over to the other woods and see what I could do about the crows.

I could tell by their talk that they had a great horned owl cornered in some tree and were doing their best to do him in.

Owls and crows are mortal enemies. The owls swoop down and kill a roosting crow at night when the crow can't see to fly. In the daytime, the crows do the same to the owl when he is at a disadvantage.

I drew closer to the battle, still undetected, with my shotgun ready.

Life as I Lived It

My first thoughts were that maybe I would get a shot at the owl and that would bring everything to a halt, but I was soon to discover that my plans were about to change.

As I crept closer still undetected and coming into range of my little Winchester 20 gauge. I, to this day, still don't know what was going through that owl's mind, when he spotted me and flew directly to me, landing on a bare tree limb directly above me. The crows came also, swooping, diving, clawing and pecking at the owl as he sat there ducking and dodging them as best as he could.

I thought to myself, that owl is either committing suicide or gambling on my help in some strange way. At that point, an aggressive, sassy crow landed on a limb out in front of the owl and started giving the owl a piece of his mind in no certain terms.

35 or 40 to one is pretty unfair odds was my thinking as the shotgun came to bear on the sassy crow, blowing him to pieces. All was silent as the crow fell to the earth.

The owl looked down, not moving a muscle, as he watched me reload. The shotgun came to bear again, searching for a second target, the crows scattered quickly, seeing that I meant business.

The owl just sat there, watching the crows fly out of sight, then he looked down at the dead crow and then at me. It was like a professional courtesy between two hunters

Richard W. Block

who happened to share the same hunting grounds. Then, without a sound, he glided away out of sight.

I never hunted those woods again, but if I had, I would bet the first thing on the crows mind, would be to let that damn owl alone if they see him again!!

THE PORCUPINE

I used to go to Michigan every year in the 1970's for the opening day of deer hunting season, which was November 15th, rain, shine or snow.

It was like an invading army of orange clad hunters of all ages, traveling north from the populated bottom of the state to the upper part where they had places to say and hunt.

It's so very interesting, how the wildlife has no fear of human beings, when they are only around them a week or two out of the whole year.

I've had birds eat from my hand many times and even sit on my rifle barrel as if it were a tree branch. I guess the feeling you get at these times can only be described as bonding, man and beast.

This brings me to this story.

During one hunting trip to Michigan, in the Grayling area, the neighbor invited a couple of our party, to hunt on his property. His name was Bill M. and he was a good friend as well as a great woodsman. He took us on a tour of his woods to find some good spots to hunt.

There was a big sand pit away into the woods, which I thought looked promising, so I stayed behind and let the others go on their way. As I stood there looking around and enjoying the peace and quiet, I heard the sound of claws on tree bark. Something was descending down a tree across the pit. What could it be, I wondered?

I hurried to the area where I heard the noise. I thought maybe it was a raccoon or squirrel and I would meet him as he reached the bottom of the tree and see what reaction it would have, maybe scare the heck out of it, just for fun.

Usually an animal will scurry back up the tree to safety, when a human approaches, but not this critter. He just kept coming on down and stopped at about eye level and looked me over with his own curious eyes. It was a porcupine. He was the first I had ever encountered up close and personal.

I thought my presence would scare him. But no, I could sense no fear on his part and that he was thinking I should be the scared one. After getting his fill of looking me over, he must have determined I was harmless and continued descending down the tree, reaching the ground and brushing me aside as he walked by.

I thought, now wait a minute. I'm not done with you yet. So, I picked up a stick and went up to him, at which point he stopped and looked up at me. He was giving me this "what do you want now look". I took the stick and gently pet him on his back, stroking his many quills that I knew

Life as I Lived It

that I dare not touch with my hand. He just stood there taking it all in.

After I had enough petting entertainment, I stopped and he began on his merry way again. He seemed to be heading for a big hole in the ground, a den of some sort, I suppose.

I ran ahead and stood in the entrance of the hole so he couldn't go in. As he approached the den he again stopped. He looked up at me with this "get out of my way look, you idiot, don't you know who I am?" At that point, I stepped aside and he then continued into the hole and disappeared from sight.

As I stood there looking at the empty hole in the ground entrance, I said to myself, "Ha, so that was a porcupine." Now if you put yourself in the other guy's shoes so to speak, he was probably thinking to himself, "Hugh, so that was a human being!"

Porcupine quills are greatly sought after by people who make jewelry or box coverings or other items that you will find in many shops that cater to tourists. The porcupines in Michigan have an exceptionally colored quill that is also sought after by fisherman that make their own flies for trout.

The quills are hollow and air filled, they don't shoot them, one has to come in physical contact with them to be impaled by them. Dogs usually get a few quills in their face when they try to attack a porcupine for the first time, after that they know better. The best way to get a quill out is to snip it in half to deflate it, and then pull it out. It's easier and less painful that way. And now you know!!

THE PROBLEM

One summer day my family was visiting my wife's parents in Cincinnati. They lived in a subdivision at the end of a cul-de-sac, French for "dead end".

While we were there, the next door neighbor came to the door and asked if I knew anything about animals. I said that I know pretty much, why do you ask? She said she had a really big problem at her house, that there was a big skunk stuck in her wall in the garage. I said, "okay I'll take a look if you like."

So we went next door to the garage and upon entering, I could see the tail of a skunk sticking out of the drywall at the floor level.

At that time, I was driving my 1963 Ford truck that had a utility bed with compartments on each side in which I carried my work tools. As luck would have it, I had one small compartment that was empty. It was on the passenger side in the very back, behind the rear wheel.

I told the neighbor lady that a skunk usually can't spray if his hind legs are not on the ground. But, to play it safe, she

Life as I Lived It

had better stand far away when I pull the skunk out. I can't guarantee what might happen.

I put on some gloves, just in case the skunk might try to bite me and then I got a grip on that tail sticking out of the wall. You know a skunk can be a strong animal when it comes to resisting force. So I started pulling and the skunk kept resisting. I kept his tail in a downward position because I knew he couldn't spray me with his tail down

Finally, he pulled free and I ran for the truck holding the skunk by his tail while the onlookers gasped at the sight. I opened the door to the bottom rear box and tossed in the skunk, slamming the door behind him. Well, that went well, I thought and the neighbor lady couldn't thank me enough. I thought, yeah, well she is not the one who is going to have to get him out of the box once I get back home!

So, later in the afternoon we were on our way home when I remembered that a bunch of the adults from the Boy Scout troop in Aurora were tearing down a couple of small buildings to get the materials to use to build something else.

I stopped by to see how things were coming along. It was a hot day and the guys were working up a good sweat as they gathered around my truck. I said to John R. through the truck window, "you look like you could use a cold beer". John said, "I sure could"! It was then I said, "right back there in the bottom box, help yourself!" I couldn't see the look on his face in my mirror, but I bet it was a Kodak moment when he came face to face with that skunk!

Richard W. Block

Everyone was laughing when he came back to the window. I don't remember the exact names he called me, but it only added to the laughter.

When I got home I left the door open and the skunk let himself out and went on his merry way I suppose. Skunks are a night animal you know.

P.S. Now that you know the word cul-de-sac means "dead end" in French, have you ever wondered what a "Noel" is? We sing songs about the First Noel at Christmas. What the heck is a Noel? Noel is the French word for Christmas. Now it makes sense doesn't it?

THE SHREW

When I was in my teens in the early 1960's, we had an unique little house guest we called "The Shrew", because that is what it was.

If you have no idea what a shrew is, I'll enlighten you.

A shrew is a member of the rodent family. It is just a little smaller than a mouse. It has a long snout like a mole does, except it has many needle like teeth, like a shark. It has a dense, short, furry grey coat with a bobtail. If it were larger in size, it would be the most ferocious warm blooded animal on earth. They are very aggressive, smart and energetic.

Where he came from, no one knew, he just showed up one day and stayed for a few months and then one day, he was gone, never to be seen again.

It's funny you know, how a person's first reaction to seeing a little mouse like rodent in your home is to kill it. Get rid of it. Get it out of here!

Well, not so, with the shrew. He earned his keep, and for this, he was allowed to stay.

My sister had a miniature poodle dog. His feed bowl sat in the kitchen, on the floor beside the kitchen sink. We always kept Purina dog chow in the bowl for her dog. We always bought the granulated dog chow that was about the size of a man's thumb nail and hard as a rock.

About once a week, the shrew would show up and lay in his supply of dog food for the week. Whoever saw him first, would announce, "The shrew is back and he is stocking up for the week."

We would all grab a chair and sit near the dog's bowl to watch.

He would appear from behind the water heater, look around to see if everyone was seated and then go to work.

He would go over to the dog food bowl and zip right up the side of the bowl to the rim, grab a granule of dog food in his mouth and then zip behind the water heater to some hiding place where he would store it and then return for another chunk. It was amazing that he could even climb the slanted sides of that anti-tip dog dish, but even more amazing was the fact that the granulated chunks of dog food were huge, as compared to his own body size! It reminded me of a seal with a huge beach ball balanced on the tip of his nose.

The shrew would run back and forth for about an hour, stocking up for the week. I guess he was a good judge of

Life as I Lived It

character. He seemed to sense that we were friendly and meant him no harm.

In trade for our friendship, food and shelter, he performed a service. He rid our house of mice, not that we had a lot of them, but certain times of the year, when the river would rise, the rodent population would be driven to higher ground, which included our house.

The shrew was a blood thirsty professional killer and he enjoyed his work because he was good at it.

I had this metal box mouse trap that you wound up like a clock. I could catch as many as fifteen mice in a setting. The trap had a tunnel through it, with a trigger platform, that when a mouse entered it and stepped on the trigger platform, it revolved and dropped the mouse into a holding chamber, leaving him unharmed, but captured.

The shrew would wait until there were captive mice in the trap and then he would purposely enter the trap and be dropped in with the mice at which time he would kill them all! I saw him kill three mice in only seconds! After his work was done he would rattle the trap and sit patiently for me to come and let him out. We had a good working relationship.

One day I heard a commotion outside our house. I went outside to see what was going on. I could hear the shrew screeching from around the corner of the house. As I turned the corner of the house I saw a stray cat fighting with the shrew. The shrew was standing upright on his hind legs, screeching in defiance at the cat. Every time the cat would swat at the shrew, the shrew would bite a chunk out of his paw.

The odds looked a little uneven to me! Maybe that is why, he was making so much noise. He was probably trying to get my attention, so my half of the working relationship, would come into play. Joe Namath would have been proud of the field goal I kicked that day, with a cat of course!

That should teach him not to mess with any of my family!!!

THE SKY TURN

One summer in the late 1980's, my family and I were on vacation in Virginia Beach. We were staying in a campground on the south end. It was a typical tourist type campground with a swimming pool, recreational room, evening entertainment, an office and gateway with American and Canadian flags everywhere and a camp store.

It's amazing how many Canadians go south for vacations. I've met many and some of them only spoke French! That's okay with me anyway, I just use a lot of hand gestures and I get along fine. One afternoon we were poking around in the camp store and I came across this book that captured my interest.

If you have never been in a camp store, it's a place that has everything to do with camping for sale and a lot of just plain silly things that won't sell anywhere else.

On this occasion, the book in question was all about boomerangs and it even included a boomerang as well. The oversized book was bearing a blue and white cover with the boomerang fastened inside. The title of the book was "The Boomerang Book" and it boasted of the "sky turn" boomerang, the only machine made boomerang in the world.

Most all boomerangs are handmade is the rule of thumb, so it seems.

I thumbed through the book and it sparked my curiosity to no end. It was also very comical! It was a whole insight into something that I knew absolutely nothing about. So I bought it!

It was great reading. It started out with man's philosophy, that when you throw something away, it goes there and stays. It doesn't come back. It had a cartoon of a man sitting at his desk throwing wadded up sheets of paper at a waste can across the room, some going in and some lying on the floor all around it.

I remember a cartoon where a crowd of people were standing on a busy street corner, looking at an unconscious man lying on the sidewalk with a lump on his head and a boomerang lying on the ground close to him and among the crowd of people stood a kangaroo thinking "I wonder if that was meant for me?" This cartoon was meant to dispel the belief that a boomerang is a weapon or a hunting tool, the same as a tennis ball is, for playing tennis.

The big and amazing difference is that a boomerang is aerodynamically designed to fly in a circular pattern and return to the point of launch, allowing the thrower to catch it, if he wishes!

Life as I Lived It

After reading the book and all of the explanations of what makes a boomerang comes back, I began to believe that it might actually work!

So, I removed the "sky turn" boomerang from inside the book and layed it flat on a smooth surface to see if the ends of the boomerang turned up 10 degrees from the flat surface, as the specifications in the book called for, which they did. Then I looked at the smooth beveled edges for nicks or dents that might hurt its flying capabilities and there were none. It looks fine to me, I thought. Let's see what it will do!

Rule no. 1 in the book was that you had to have a minimum of 75 yards of clear area to throw it in.

Rule no. 2 in the book was, never break rule no. 1!

The throwing instructions said to hold the boomerang in your right hand with the tip in the center of your palm and the beveled edges of the boomerang on the left side of it. Close your hand, holding it in your fist firmly and throw it as if you were throwing a baseball at an imaginary target ten feet off the ground, at an 80 degree angle, not quite straight over your head, being aware to flex your wrist quickly, to give the boomerang plenty of spin as you released it. Sounds easy, doesn't it?

The hard part though, is to throw it with enough spin, to bring the aerodynamics into play, that will make the boomerang fly in its predetermined flight pattern and return to the sender, you!

Richard W. Block

With a little practice and a good boomerang you can get pretty darn good.

They are an amazing instrument of flight.

A funny story: I had a boomerang laying in my vehicle one day when I had stopped by my neighbors house to catch up on the local "gossip" so to say and he saw it laying there and made the remark that he didn't believe that those things could possibly work, that they were some kind of joke and he would have to see it work, to believe it.

Well it happened to be a very calm day and a large open field was nearby.

It's ideal if there is less than 3 miles per hour of wind and the best way to tell that is to open a book in the middle and lay it down on the ground. If the wind flips the pages over, you have more than a 3 mile per hour wind.

So, we walked over to the field. Ralph stood beside me as I explained to him that I was going to throw it to the right, it would fly in a wide circle coming around to left where it would climb high and then come in at a dive like a hawk after a mouse, so you had better watch out. Turning to my right I launched my boomerang and away it went, spinning in its circular flight pattern and climbing in altitude to make its dive for home. I kept telling Ralph to keep his eye on it, it's coming for you!

Down it came like a dive bomber with its target in sight. Ralph dove to his left on the ground as the boomerang hit the ground beside me, exactly on the spot where Ralph had been standing only seconds before! Ralph picked himself up and said, "well you certainly made a believer out of me!" Then we headed for the house in search of a cold beer.

There was a disappointing statement in the "boomerang book" for some people and it stated that if you are left hander, .forget it! You are not capable of throwing a boomerang, unless, you can find someone who can make you a left handed boomerang!

I have owned and flown scores of handmade boomerangs that are impressive to see in flight, but I always think back to when I bought that darn "boomerang book" with the wooden "sky turn" inside and I wonder, where in hell did I put that darn book, I can't find it anywhere!

THE TRUMPET

One day as I was leaving the scout camp, I noticed a yard sale by the highway. I am always looking for bargains, so I stopped to see what might be there. The only thing that caught my interest was a silver trumpet in its case. I noticed that there was a blue ribbon first place medal from the Indiana State Music competition.

I thought, this must be a really great trumpet, if it took first place. Unfortunately, I didn't know how to play it, but the price was right. I asked the people about it, but they knew little of its history, they just wanted to be shed of it. So, I bought it.

I stored it away along with a variety of other instruments that I had accumulated over the years.

I thought that maybe my children might want to learn to play them and be in the school band someday.

When my oldest son, Richard, got old enough to be in the school band, I showed him the silver trumpet and the medal and told him this is a champion musical instrument

Life as I Lived It

and that if he learned to play it, it would take him places he couldn't imagine in the world of music.

He joined the band and played first chair all through school. When he graduated and went off to the Military Academy, the trumpet was again stored away.

As time passed, I was blessed with grandchildren and they were also interested in music and playing instruments.

One day my grandson, Josh, called on the phone and asked if I had any trumpets stored away. He wanted one to play in his school band, now that he was old enough.

I said, "Sure, come on over and pick one out." I told him that I had 3 trumpets and a cornet to choose from.

I showed him 2 brass trumpets and the silver one also. He seemed to fancy the silver one, so I told him of its history and if he chose to take it I would expect no less than first chair and great accomplishments out of it and him. It will take you places if you learn to master it and play it well.

As time, passed, Josh learned to play it well and he was first chair. Then he was asked to play solos at concerts and he did great. Special competitions and band groups came his way.

The school band leader took an interest in this silver trumpet that seemed to out class all the others.

He told Josh that this trumpet is no ordinary trumpet. It's not a beginner's trumpet, it's a higher class trumpet than a beginners. That's why it plays and sounds so well.

Richard W. Block

I didn't know there were different grades of trumpets.

Last Christmas Josh got a professional grade top of the line trumpet from Santa. He's really proud of it, but he doesn't want to let go of the silver trumpet that got him where he is, just yet.

It's hard to let go, but there are other grandchildren who may someday be waiting their turn to see where an old yard sale trumpet might take them!

THE WALLET

One cold winter day, my Dad took me with him to run an errand across town to one of his friend's home.

I was about 8 years old at the time and there was snow on the ground, a couple of inches deep from the night before.

Dad pulled up and parked in front of his friend's house on Stuart Street. It was a place my family went just about every week to relax, visit and play cards.

As I walked around the car to my Dad's side, I stumbled upon something in the snow.

I picked the object up and shook off the snow, revealing a brown leather wallet.

"Look" I said, "Look what I found", as I handed the wallet to Dad. Dad opened the wallet and looked at the name and address inside. Then Dad said, "I know this man and he will be glad to get his wallet back. It has all of his papers in it and most of his paycheck in cash I imagine".

It had over $60.00 n it. That was a good amount of money in 1956.

A short time later, we were on our way home, when we passed by our turn and kept going. "Where are we going Dad?" I asked. "We are going to return the wallet" he said.

Dad pulled up in front of a house unfamiliar to me. As Dad climbed out of the car, he said "Well, come on, you found it and you get to return it!"

We walked to the front door of the house. As Dad knocked on the door, he handed me the wallet and said, "Here ya go. Talk to the man when he comes".

The door opened and a big man appeared. I said, as I handed him the wallet. "Here, I found this and I think it is yours".

I was a bashful little fellow and I said no more. The man briefly thumbed through the wallet and said, "Yes, it is mine and in good order too!" He thanked me and praised me for being such an honest young man and going out of our way to return his wallet.

I know in my heart that my Dad was beaming with pride for what I had done. Of course, my Dad was a big part of it, but stayed in the background of the event. That was his way of teaching me things. Then the man handed me two dollars! That is a lot of money, especially when candy bars only cost a nickel! That's 40 candy bars I thought. I thanked the man very much!

On the way home Dad asked me what was I going to do with my reward money! I said, "Stop at the store Dad, I want some candy!"

THE WAY I SEE IT!

I grew up in a small town where everyone was prejudice toward races and religions. Everyone was white in my community.

As a child, I grew up being the same way because I didn't know anything else.

After I graduated High School, I took a job in the big city as an assistant manager in a McDonalds Restaurant. It was there that I learned the error of my ways.

I turned my train of thoughts to cars. There are all kinds of cars. Some are big and some are small. There are more colors than you can count and more configurations than you can imagine. Some are good and some are bad and some last long and some only a short time.

Still, they are basically all cars.

It's the same with people, just as it is with cars.

How do you see it?

Americans are a strange breed of people. If we are not fighting with foreigners in distant lands, then we are fighting among ourselves!

What do you think is wrong with us? Do you think we will all learn the errors of our ways?

THE WHISTLE

Once upon a time in the late 1960's into the early 1970's, I worked in a distillery in the little town of Lawrenceburg, Indiana, about five miles away from my home. It was one of several distilleries owned by the well known company based in New York. It employed about two thousand people at its peak in our area alone.

The great thing about working in a job that employs thousands, is the variety of people you get to spend time with, that come from all walks of life. They can teach a young man many things about life, if he is hungry to learn and if they have the patience to teach him what they know or what talent they might have.

I worked in the bottling plant which is where the whiskey is bottled, labeled, cased and shipped or warehoused.

I knew hundreds of my co-workers. Many of them have passed on now, but there are those that I will never forget that enriched my life many times with their, stories, tips, words of wisdom, talents and just plain friendship.

Life as I Lived It

One of these people was a small fellow by the name of Bill Winters, whom everyone called "Willie". Bill was a relief man. His job was to come around and take your place on the job for fifteen minutes, a couple times before lunch and a couple times after, rotating from worker to worker each time all day long. I usually worked on a bottling line with a lot of people, so Bill was near me often, several times a day.

One day, Bill was trying to get someone's attention and couldn't make himself heard above the noise of the machinery and the sounds of everything else in motion, so he whistled loud to get his point across.

I said to him, "how do you whistle like that? I've tried to learn how to do that all my life and could never master the technique." Bill replied, "It's not hard anyone can do it, it just takes a little practice and finding the right way that is right for you.

"What do you mean by that?" I asked. Then he proceeded to show me several different ways to whistle loud like he does.

Now Bill could simply curl his tongue and whistle his way, but I couldn't do it like that, so he said that it was okay because there was a couple of other ways you could do it by using your fingers to help in the process.

I found that using my little finger on each hand in the corners of my mouth forming a "v" as they came together on my tongue yielded the best results for me. I practiced and practiced trying every angle of the "v" until I was finally able to get the loud sound that I wanted.

Richard W. Block

Can you hear me now?

I've always considered learning to whistle loud like Bill as one of the most valuable things that I learned at that place on the road to life's many lessons.

Bill has passed on by many years I am sure, but in a way it's kind of a tribute to him every time I use the whistle he taught me to call in my children or get someone's attention because his whistle lives on in me.

I think of Bill often and also the many people like him, who have taught me many things along the way in my life and I thank them for their time and patience that helped make me the person that I am today.

TOM

When I worked for McDonald's Restaurants, we had a store in downtown Cincinnati that I had to service whenever they had equipment problems.

If you have ever been downtown in a big city during the week and tried to find a place to park, well good luck!

I always felt picked on when I was parked in a regular parking place on the street. It always seemed like the meter maid was standing by the meter with the parking ticket already filled out, waiting for the meter to expire and then slapping it on my windshield before I could get there to drop another coin in the meter. I swear those parking meters ran faster than my watch!

I was darn tired of getting parking tickets on my company maintenance truck every time I was there.

One day I was cruising the block looking for a place to park and there just wasn't any to be had. Just around the corner from the restaurant was a truck unloading zone that was usually vacant and was big enough for two or three trucks or vans, so what the heck, I will park there and hope I don't get a ticket.

As I took my tools from my truck and started to leave, a man in a wheel chair spoke to me and asked if I was going to be gone very long. I told him I had some work to do at McDonalds around the corner and I wasn't sure how long it would take.

This unloading zone was in front of another restaurant/night club with six stories of apartments above it.

Tom introduced himself and told me he lived in the apartment building here.

I introduced myself and we struck up a conversation. I had seen Tom there before but had no occasion to meet or talk to him. As we talked, people would pass by and greet Tom and it seemed like most everyone who passed had something to say to him. He seemed to be quite popular or something.

I told him of my parking ticket problem and he said that when I come downtown, to park right here and he would see to it that no one bothered my truck and I would get no tickets. I kind of thought that was strange because he only just met me but what the heck, it was okay with me.

From then on, I parked in that spot and Tom was always there in his wheelchair, come rain or shine, hot or cold.

I would visit with Tom whenever I had the time and I got to know him a little better each time. Tom was a street person, he was always there and he knew everyone and everything that went on in his little world.

I would give him coupons for free food at McDonalds and he would keep my truck under a watchful eye.

At times he would point out various people to me and say, "Do you see that girl there? She is only sixteen and she is a prostitute. She takes guys back in the alley across the street to do business". "See that man there? That is her pimp; he watches over her and is never far away".

These people looked like regular people. I could not tell them from anyone else in dress manner. "You see that guy over there?" He would point and say, "That is an undercover cop. These streets are well protected whether you know it or not".

Tom never ceased to impress me and I never got another ticket either.

It has been many years and Tom is no longer there anymore. I suppose he has passed on like many of my friends and I suppose a lot of people miss him too.

TORNADO

In the Spring of 1974, I experienced my first tornado while working as a manager at the McDonald's in Western Hills, a suburb of Cincinnati, Ohio. It was known as store number 696 by the McDonald's Corporation and Western Hills McDonald's, by the franchise owner for whom I worked.

I was working the night shift, which was 4:00 p.m. to closing, which was generally 11:00 p.m. with another hour and a half of inventory and paper work, along with crew clean-up of the restaurant.

I had just started my shift and already, I was getting phone calls from concerned crew people, wanting to know if they should report for work or stay home, because of the repeated tornado warnings broadcast on the T.V. and radio.

My advice was to come to work, that it was highly unlikely that we would see any tornados. Besides, our store had a basement with concrete flooring above on the main floor. It was like a bunker and could withstand a direct hit by a tornado, with little or no consequences.

Life as I Lived It

It was a nice sunny day and everything was quite normal until about 5:30 p.m., when it began to hail. The hail stones were quite large, not the normal pea size, but bigger than an average marble, but smaller than a golf ball! They were coming down like bullets, pelting everything in sight.

Four teenage boys, who thought they should be somewhere else, unwisely ran out to where their car was parked, but the driver had previously locked the doors and they couldn't get inside the car until he found the keys in his pockets to unlock the doors!

It was a comical sight. Everyone in the restaurant was chuckling as they watched the boys hopping around, as the hail stones pelted them, like a bunch of Mexican jumping beans. Another young man came running inside from the parking lot, wearing a football helmet, his way of braving the elements!

That too, was pretty funny; according to the laughs put forth by the watching customers.

All of the excitement soon passed, along with the hail storm. I didn't know that this was only the end of phase one.

Had I experienced a tornado before, I would have known that tornados are usually preceded by a hail storm before they hit.

It was now around 6:00 p.m. and the peak of our "supper rush".

Richard W. Block

The holding bin was full of food and the customers were four deep at the front counter, ordering their evening meal.

All was normal until a young boy, standing in line, in the all glass dinning lobby, shouted out, as he pointed his finger and arm at the side lobby glass, "look!! There's a tornado!"

Sure enough, there it was, advancing toward us like a whirling Tasmanian Devil! A huge funnel cloud, the likes of which, I had never seen, was coming closer and closer at a seemingly slow pace, chewing and belching up debris like some hungry beast.

I learned later, that of the five tornados that passed through the area that day, this one had crossed the Ohio River from Kentucky, moving Northward through the little river community of Saylor Park, up South Road toward Western Hills and through Mack and Dent, Ohio in a northwesterly sweep.

I now stood in the lobby, watching its progress. Customers cars were screaming out of our parking lot and the lobby was empty except for a family of four who were packing up their two children in preparation of doing the same. The man came over, and stood beside me as we watched. He asked me if I thought the tornado would come this far?

Being the country boy that I always was, I told him "no", as I pointed out the westward direction of the cloud it was attached to, was drifting. "I think the tornado will have to turn right and go west, as well," I said.

The man's wife, with kids in tow, shouted, "we'll be in the car! Are you coming?" He replied in a calm voice, "no, I think I'm going to sit down and eat my quarter pounder". And he did, as his wife and kids watched from their car. Then he left as well.

There I stood, all alone in an empty lobby with a holding bin full of fresh cooked and wrapped McDonald's product. What a waste I thought.

As I looked through the glass at the tornado, the people from our neighboring camera shop were standing outside in front of me, taking pictures of the tornado with cameras they had grabbed from their store shelves and just slapped some film in. The price tags were still dangling from the cameras!

I had previously sent my crew people to the basement just in case things went the wrong way. One of the crew ventured top side and asked if it was okay to come out?

The tornado did make it's turn to the west as I had thought it might, so I gave the all clear and everyone soon appeared, a little excited but keeping their calm about them, as I knew they would. I had a well trained crew and I was proud of them always.

I remarked to them, "well we've got plenty of food but no customers. But, what's really amazing is that we still have power and everything is normal. You would think that a tornado, cutting a half mile wide path, would sooner or later destroy the power line."

Richard W. Block

At that very instant, the lights went out and all power was lost! Can you believe it? Not only had we lost all power and lights, it was also evening and rapidly getting dark.

"We are closing up", I remarked. "I predict, no return of electric for a long time, so let's do all the closing procedures as usual, with the exception of opening any freezer or refrigerator doors. They must remain sealed to keep in the temperature as long as the equipment can keep it."

And so, we were soon closed and I found myself all alone in a dark McDonald's, sitting in my desk chair with my sawed off double barrel shotgun across my lap, watching the flashlights beaming all around in the shopping mall across the street. Looters or employees, I know not.

With all the electric off, there was a lot of looting and break-ins, because there were no working alarms.

I found great comfort in that shotgun. I only started carrying it after I received 10 stitches in my head during a hold-up attempt. It's interesting how people go out of their way, to get out of your way, when you carry the right tool! All I knew, was that whoever broke into McDonald's tonight, would be found there in the morning!

A fireman from the fire department stopped by looking for food donations for the rescue workers and people in need. Boy, did he stop at the right place! We fixed him right up! I was glad, not to have thrown all that food out!

Much later, I passed through Saylor Park on my way home. There were huge trees across all four lanes of highway, with

Life as I Lived It

only a small zig zag path, through which a single car could pass, cut by the firemen who had been working there for hours.

It's amazing, the things that tornados do, such as removing the top of a house, but not disturbing any of the contents, which was the case of one of our company executives.

One day, about a month later, one of the crew guys asked me if I thought the next door camera shop people had gotten any good pictures? He was working on a school project and thought the tornado would be a good subject.

We were in a slow period of the day, so I said, "run next door and see what they have."

He soon returned with a handful of 8x12 pictures of everything, you couldn't imagine!

"They have a huge selection of everything, including aftermath photos for a dollar a piece in 8x12 sizes," he said.

There was one photo that really caught my eye. It was the photo taken by the cameraman who stood outside in front of me as I watched through the lobby glass, as the tornado approached McDonald's. It was as if I had taken the picture myself, as I saw it.

needless to say, I bought a copy framed it, and still have it on display in my home. Awesome!!!

U.F.O.'S

Now there's a touchy subject for you. Are there really U.F.O's? By U.F.O's, I am referring to spacecrafts from another planet, piloted by intelligent beings. But of course they would be intelligent beings. They evidently built and navigate their spacecrafts to our plant!

Does our Government have proof by way of wreckage and bodies from these visitors? I think so.

It's funny how people look at you like you are some kind of deranged person when you express opinions or relate experiences to them that they just can't or won't believe. When people ask you if you believe in U.F.O.'s and you say "yes" and also have you ever seen one and you say "yes" again, they instantly begin to think you are definitely a nut case or some kind of liar.

One morning in the early hours before daylight, about 4:00 a.m., I was sitting in my car with my girlfriend in front of her house. She lived near Aurora, Indiana along the Ohio River. Her house and driveway overlooked the river which was about 300 years away, just across the road.

Life as I Lived It

As we sat there talking in the dark, a "flying saucer" came zipping up and hovered over the river at tree top level, which was right out in front of my car. It reminded me of a low silhouette top hat with chase pattern lights going around and around where the hat band would be.

I said, "Look at that! What is that?" We watched as it hovered there for a short time, then it zipped instantly, like the click of your fingers to a position over the hills in Kentucky about 10 miles away and hovered there for a bit before disappearing like the turning off of a light switch.

Some years later, I was deer hunting with some friends one November evening. When it got too dark to shoot, we all met at the car to begin our trip home. As we were unloading our guns, I made the remark that I had noticed an unusually bright star to the west and did anyone else notice it also? Tim said, "Yes, you mean that one there", as he pointed at it. "That's no star," he said, "I've been watching it all evening and it's been moving around."

At that very instant, it began moving as we watched. It came toward us, and as it approached, it was very noticeable that it was triangular in shape and made a pulsating left-right jog flight pattern, as if dodging something.

I had a telescopic sight on my gun and as I put my gun to my shoulder to get a better look at it, my hunting buddies mobbed me yelling don't shoot at it. By the time I was able to free myself and my gun from them, it had moved too far away to get a good look at.

Richard W. Block

I was mad as hell and still am when I think of how they cheated me of getting a good close look at the U.F.O. The odd thing about the sightings is that neither one made any sounds. No engine noise, nothing!

Recently, on one of the TV programs, they were showing pictures of supposed U.F.O.'s that different people had taken and sent in, or the program had compiled. The program was asking the question, were these real or concocted photos of supposed U.F.O.'s? One of the photos was unmistakably the same spacecraft I first saw hovering over the Ohio River in those early morning hours many years ago.

After all these years of wonderment, someone had actually taken a photograph of the same craft I had seen. It really made me feel good to know I was not alone in what I had seen.

Just think. If it takes millions of light years of travel, just to leave our own galaxy, then where do these U.F.O.'s come from? How could they reach here alive? Scientists point their fingers at Mars and Venus, but these planets are either too hot or too cold to sustain life, due to their distance from the sun. Earth is just the right distance and orbit for sustaining life as everyone well knows. So, where can the U.F.O.'s come from? I have a theory. What if earth has a sister planet? An unseen planet, following the same exact orbit as Earth, but only on the opposite side of the circular orbit, with the sun always in between, hiding it from view. An earth number 2, with the same life sustaining capabilities as we have here. Twin Planets!

Think about it.

These U.F.O.'s have to come from within our own galaxy.

Where would you point your finger?

Think again..........

V-65 MAGNA

Somewhere back in the 1980's era, Honda came out with their v-65 Magna motorcycle.

They would show T.V. commercials, advertising the V-65 Magna and how it could go from zero to sixty in a matter of only a few seconds. It really looked fast on the television. They always had a small light weight Japanese rider doing the test ride, so I always thought that maybe that small rider was also helping to boost the speed figures.

I always liked the Honda motorcycles. I have had five Harleys before and they were just too high maintenance for me to enjoy them as much as I did my virtually maintenance free Hondas.

My friend John T. has a motorcycle shop that he started in the basement of his home and bloomed into a Honda dealership. I was at his shop one day, for who knows what, when I passed by one of the new V-65 Magna parked out front along the walkway.

I asked John if that was his V-65 test ride bike parked out front. (I was making a joke). John said, "No, that is

Life as I Lived It

a factory recall, Honda thinks one of their automated welders missed a weld joint on the frame, but I cannot see anything wrong with the weld joints. If you would like to try it out, take it for a ride but, I caution you to look at the speedometer once in a while. It will fool you."

Little did I know that I was just about to get an education and the ride of my life! "The key is in it" John said, as I turned for the door.

There it sat, in its entire splendor, the V-65 Magna, supposedly the fastest thing on two wheels to date.

I grabbed the handle bars and threw my leg over the saddle seat, turned the key and fired that baby up. It had a sound of some real power as it warmed up.

I flipped up the kickstand and slowly putted from the parking area onto the road in front of the shop which led out to the main highway. I took it slow until I reached the stop sign.

I pulled out onto the highway which was straight as an arrow for about a mile and just sat there riving it up and thinking about the T.V. commercial and how fast the little rider could make it go. Well, let's just see what it will really do, I thought to myself.

There was no traffic in sight and the time is now. I laid forward on the gas tank, so the front wheel would stay on the ground, revved the motor up and let out on the clutch. If you have never heard of a "bat out of hell" well this was it.

The bike lunged forward throwing me back to my arms length. It was all I could do just to hang on. The V-65 was screaming down the highway so fast that I could feel the skin on my face push into the recesses of my check bones. I could not even smile; my face muscles were so flattened! I shifted to second gear and again it was all I could do to hang on. I had a tiger by the tail. I shifted to third gear and again I was fighting to hang on as I shot down the road like a bullet.

As I readied to shift to fourth gear, John's words of caution echoed in my ears, "look at the speedometer once in a while, it will fool you". So, I glanced at the speedometer, I was going 110 miles an hour and I still had three more gears to go! The V-65 has a six speed transmission and the speedometer goes up to 180 M.P.H., which at this point, I had no doubt that it would go that fast!

I immediately let go of the throttle and let it coast to a reasonable speed where I could turn around and take it back to the shop.

I parked the bike back where it had been sitting and climbed off. As I did, one of the mechanics asked me what was wrong. "What do you mean", I asked. He said that most everyone who rides that bike comes back with a big smile on their face, but you are not smiling. I said, "That is because I am too terrified to smile. The muscles in my face still have not thawed out yet".

When I went inside, John asked me how I liked the test ride.

I said it was okay and thanked him for it.

As I drove home I knew in my heart that I would never allow myself to own a bike like that because sooner or later I would get used to it and feel that I have become the master of it, as many do and it is at that point in a biker's life, when the bike usually gets you down and grinds you into the blacktop. If you are real lucky, you might live to tell about it and show off your scars. There is a biker's saying that goes, "you ain't rode, till you been throw'd".

My son, Mike made the mistake that I avoided. He bought the bike that was too fast.

My father always told me that, "if you ride a motorcycle like a gentlemen you will have no problems".

I passed this same advice along to my children.

Mike didn't pay any attention that was his final mistake.

VACATIONS

I always used to make the statement that someday when I retire, I am going to travel to faraway places and see the things that I have never had the time to see, because I will have the time to spare when I retire, to go and do what I please.

One day, I made that statement to one of my friends, Larry C., who is a down to earth, common sense person, who refrained, "That is a bunch of crap Dick, it will never happen. You will be too old and crippled or too broke to go and do what you want when or if you ever retire. If you want to do those things, you have to do it now, while you still can. If you really want to do those things, you have to make and take the time to do it, or it will probably never happen", Larry said.

The more I thought about it, the more I realized he was right.

I owned a time share condo in the Bahamas for ten years and I had never even seen the place. My relatives would go there and stay and enjoy the place. They would show me

Life as I Lived It

pictures of it when they returned home and tell me about it, but I had never been there to see the place for myself.

So, my first step was to get a passport and then go and see the condo.

I didn't really need a passport to go to the Bahamas at that time. A driver's license and birth certificate would get you through customs ok, but an American passport did the job much faster. It is really amazing how quickly that little blue book with the gold American eagle on the cover will open doors for you, while others have to go through lengthy process to get where it only takes seconds to go with that passport.

My condo was right on the ocean, facing East, with the beach only fifty yards from the door. It was beautiful and it only took me ten years to get there! What a waste of time! I should have been coming here for ten years, I thought.

In comparison, Freeport and Nassau are cities and Abbaco is country.

There is no crime there I learned and the people are so nice. It is just a different way of life. It is one of the only places where I could ever consider living full time, if I had to.

I had learned long ago to take a tour if you really want to know the history, customs and layout of the place.

A good example is that I had visited Mackinac Island many times over a period of years. I wandered all over the island, looking at everything and seeing the sights. One trip, I was too tired to go wandering around everywhere, so I took a carriage tour and learned more in a few hours then I did in many years of not knowing what I was looking at, while wandering around on my own!

I met a lot of people from all over the world in the Bahamas and made many friends. I learned much history and customs. The one thing that I learned there that I still use when I am in a tropical area is how to tell if a coconut is ripe and how to open it. I bring some home each time I can and let the scouts and the schools locally have a go at them. It is a very entertaining program, if not hilarious! Just watch those kids try to get them open.

Getting back on track, the Bahamas was the first of an every year, go somewhere vacation trip spree.

We, my wife and I, have gone to Freeport, Abbaco Island several times, Jamaica,

Amsterdam, Germany twice, Austria, Bavaria, Switzerland, Hawaii, Alaska and Cancun to name a few places.

It helps to know a little bit of the languages too. The more prepared you are, the less problems you are likely to have.

My friend Larry was right and I am glad I took his advice.

Take the time and do what you have to, to make your dreams come true while you are still able. That is my advice to anyone who will listen.

WATER PUDDLE

Nick U., Denny Y. and I had taken the scout troop on one of our many trips to the Eastern U.S., where we usually visited places like Washington D.C., Williamsburg, Virginia Beach, etc.

We were tooling along in our troop's school bus, going north along Virginia Beach main drag just seeing the sights.

It had rained earlier that day and there were water puddles everywhere, some of them like small lakes, they were so big.

The sun was shining. People were stirring everywhere, because the sun had come out and the weather was beautiful again.

A convertible Mustang had pulled up to the main road and was sitting at a stop sign waiting for us to pass so they could pull out and continue on.

The top was down, revealing two ladies with large sun hats on. I yelled, "Hey, watch this guys!" Everyone on the bus looked in surprise as I swerved the bus to the right, hitting the large water puddle that lay in front of the Mustang, causing a huge tidal wave of water to engulf the car, drowning everything in its path.

The ladies just sat there in disbelief as the water was draining from atop their hats and onto the floor with the rest of the water that was dripping from their soaked clothes.

Everyone in the bus was roaring laughing. Denny said, "Aren't you afraid you'll get in trouble for that?" I said, "No. Who's going to believe that a bus load of Boy Scouts did a deed like that?"

WEST POINT PINK

It was Plebe Parent weekend 1996 at the United States Military Academy, West Point, New York. That's the same difference as spring break for the upper class men and except for a few cadets on special assignments; the Academy was in the hands of the Plebes entertaining their parents.

My son, Richard, was one of these Plebes and his mother, I and his two brothers were present enjoying the program set forth by the Academy.

Think of this. The U.S.M.A. can feed 5,000 cadets and staff in 15 minutes! This is three times a day, every day.

We were gathered at Washington Hall, which is the mess hall, for the evening meal. The only difference being, each table of ten was filled with parents and their cadets, rather than all cadets. Everyone was dressed in their best. The Cadets looked smart in their uniforms of grey with the rows of brass buttons, white gloves and white pants.

Richard was positioned at the head of the table and we still argue about it to this very day, I say he hooked it with his sleeve button as he sat down and he says I bumped it as he sat down and he says I bumped it with my movie camera as I was turning to place it on the floor, but I can still vision that pitcher of red punch upside down in the middle of his lap and the look on his face when he stood and saw, to his horror, his now bright pick uniform.

Shielded by the other cadets at our table, they left without discovery, in search for another uniform to wear. Each cadet only has one dress tunic.

He returned, wearing the highest ranking upperclassman's tunic he could find! The other unaware cadets were astounded at his immediate promotion! I thought, "Oh boy!" He was already leading his class in demerits, what's a few more as the servers mopped a four table floor area. You'd have thought that was a ten gallon pitcher!

WHAT WOULD YOU DO?

It was around 4:00 P.M. and it was time to head home.

I worked for a McDonald's restaurant franchise in Cincinnati and I was in a hurry trying to beat the rush hour traffic. I had to go through the heart of the city and it was the outbound traffic on the Westside I was concerned about.

As I approached an intersection, I could see there was an accident ahead. As I passed I could see no one was hurt, but a full sized Chevy van and a Volkswagen Rabbit were hooked together. The right rear bumper corner of the Rabbit was hooked in the left front wheel well right behind the bumper corner of the Chevy van which apparently happened as both vehicles were turning at the same time in double lanes. I was glad I was inbound because the traffic was backing up and was going to get real ugly because two lanes were totally blocked.

I was driving a maintenance truck with plenty of tools so I went around the block and parked close by... I stood and watched with the policeman on the corner as a middle aged man jumped up and down on a bumper while a young

Richard W. Block

man screamed about possibly scratching his new van and an elderly man sat on the curb in dismay.

I asked, "Can I help?" He said, "Be my guest!" I returned with my 2 ton jack on wheels and started lifting the van front hoping it would release the Rabbit but it held tight. Now the young man was screaming at me. I could now see the Rabbit was in a binding angle to the van and proposed that I left the entire Rabbit on my wheeled jack and move it parallel to the van so they could release.

The young man protested louder, but the elderly man on the curb spoke up and said, "Do whatever it takes, it's my car." So I did, and they released without one tiny scratch!

I picked up my jack and left. Not one word of thanks was given, even though I knew there were many thankful people. In today's world of lawsuits and liabilities, I ask myself would I do it again. What would your answer be?

WILD GOOSE

The Boy Scout Jamborees were held every four years at Fort A.P. Hill, Virginia and we would load up our scouts on our troop bus and travel there for the event.

We usually have extra room on this particular trip, so we invited another scout troop to go with us. That pretty much filled up the bus.

The standing rule is that visiting troops are not permitted to camp within a fifty mile radius of the Jamboree because it is a National event with over one hundred thousand scouts participating So, if you are visiting, you have to stay fifty miles away, so the place doesn't get jammed up with people and traffic.

We were lucky. We found a new scout camp that was still under construction and wasn't open yet, but they would let us use the facilities for free.

A contractor had owned the property and went belly up trying to develop the place.

Richard W. Block

It had a big log cabin type lodge with two full bathrooms that we could use for showers. Outside was a row of port-o-lets by a huge lake where flocks of geese enjoyed the nice clear waters.

All the scouts were dressed in their Class A uniforms and were gathering around the bus to get ready to load up and go to the Jamboree fifty miles away.

I always drive the bus and I went to my tent to get something from my pack. While I was there I noticed I had my goose call in one of the pockets. I thought maybe I could have some fun with that later, so I slipped it into my pocket and headed toward the bus.

The bus was parked close to the port-o-lets, so I thought I had better use one quick before I got behind the driver's seat for the hour or so ride to the Jamboree.

While I was in the port-o-let, I remembered the goose call in my pocket. As I was ready to exit, I started squawking on the call and thumping around, rocking the port-o-let violently back and forth like there was a big fight going on in there. After a while, I stopped and listened.

I only heard silence. I thought, well, I guess everyone must have gotten on the bus and missed the show I just performed.

I opened the door and stepped out to a crowd of shocked faces.

I thought, this is "The Moment".

"The moment" is a fleeting moment that when it comes around, you have to be quick to say something or the moment is gone and you later think that you should have said something memorable, but didn't and now you regret letting it get away!

And so, I thought, this is "the moment"!

So I gave them a worn out tired look and said, "Wow! I thought I'd never get that goose shoved down that hole in there!"

At that, the crowd burst out in uncontrollable laughter which went on for about five minutes.

As we loaded up the bus, I overheard one of the adults in our troop, telling the Scoutmaster of the other troop that, "We have something in our troop that you don't have." "What's that?" he asked. "A Dick Block!", was the reply.

I thought to myself, gee what an endorsement!

WILLIE WONDERFUL

One of the great mysteries in my life, as a youth growing up, was what ever happened to my dog Willie Wonderful?

Willie was a shaggy, brown haired mutt who was as ornery as they come and liked to chase everything he saw.

He was just like all my other dogs, he loved me with a passion and like all my other dogs before, and I was the only person who could make him mind.

Well, one day Willie disappeared! I came home from school and there was no Willie to be found anywhere. I called and I called but no Willie came running as was the usual. Where in the heck could that little stinker be? No one seemed to know. I looked everywhere. I thought maybe he had been hit by a car or something, but he was nowhere to be found.

I thought well, he'll come home sooner or later. It was so unlike him to be gone for any length of time. Well, Willie never did come home. He just flat disappeared from the face of the earth and when something like that happened, my dad usually had something to do with it.

Life as I Lived It

I asked Dad, "Are you sure you don't know what happened to Willie?" He'd say no and that would be the end of that. I'd never had a dog just up and run off like that. It was a real mystery and it bothered me for years afterwards.

About a dozen years later I was thinking about it for some reason and I asked my Dad, "Say, do you remember that curly haired brown dog I had named Willie Wonderful?" Dad said, "Yes I remember him". I was surprised that he said he remembered him, especially out of all of the dogs that I had had in my life. I said, "Well, what ever happened to him? Surely you know". He then simply said, "I shot him". I didn't expect that answer. Dad was a dog lover if anybody was and I just couldn't believe he would do that unless it was a drastic measure.

I asked, "Well what happened? Was he hit by a car or something and you had to put him out of his misery or what?" After he gave me his answer, I wish I hadn't asked! He said, "I was going to relocate Willie to a new home, but I couldn't catch him". "What do you mean a new home?" I asked. Dad Said, "That dog was so mean and ornery that everyone in the neighborhood was afraid of being bitten. He snapped at your sister and that was the last straw. I tried my best to catch him but he was too quick and smart and I had to shoot him as a last resort."

I said, "Well, why didn't you wait for me to come home from school? I could have caught him". Dad said, "I didn't want you involved because you'd raise a fuss, so the dog had to go before you got home."

Well, that solved the mystery of a dozen years and that was answer enough, but for some reason Dad continued on in detail about Willie.

"Willie was one of the toughest dogs I have ever seen. He was in the back yard and I grabbed your mom's Winchester rifle. If I shot him once, I shot him a dozen times. He just wouldn't go down! I've never seen an animal as tough as he was, he just wouldn't hold still!" Dad said.

At that point, I stopped his talking by saying, "Gee Dad, I just wanted to solve the mystery, not to particularly know the graphic details!"

Dad did say that he buried Willie in the back yard. Nothing was ever spoken of the matter after that.

I always looked up to my Dad without fail. I knew in my heart that he felt that what he had done was necessary. Not right or wrong, just necessary.

It was a tough decision, but he was used to tough decisions, he had me to raise!

WOODLORE WITH DAD

Memories are a strange thing. They are not bound to the passing of time. You can remember a grown person as they were as a child and see them clearly in your mind's eye as if they were here now re-enacting some memorable moment all over again such as I am doing now, remembering the lesson of woodlore I taught my eldest son one mid-November day.

It was the beginning of Deer hunting season and I took my son, Richard, with me for the early morning hunt. We descended the hill leading to the creek bed where I knew the deer traveled the bank edges leaving well-worn trails. As we quietly stalked along, I pointed out different deer tracks, broken limbs from passage and nibbled vegetation showing the very recent presence of deer. Then I spotted the curious little mound of marbles. I said to my son; "look at this. What do you think this is?" He shrugged his shoulders in wonderment as he viewed the shiny green mound of marble shaped pellets, still wet from the morning dew.

Pick one up, I said and feel it. This he did. Is it warm or cold I asked? Kind of warm, Richard replied. Roll it around between your fingers. Does it feel moist? Yes was the reply. Now squeeze it. What does it look like inside? Is it green and full of fiber as well? Yes was the reply again. Now smell it. As he looked up with the foulest look on his face and saw my departing silhouette, he heard me mutter, "That's right, it's deer poop!"